THE JOURNEY™
for Kids

Liberating Your Child's Shining Potential

BRANDON BAYS

element

Element
An Imprint of HarperCollins*Publishers*
77–85 Fulham Palace Road
Hammersmith, London W6 8JB

The website address is: www.thorsonselement.com

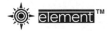

and *Element* are trademarks of
HarperCollins*Publishers* Limited

Published by Element 2003

7 9 10 8 6

Illustrations by David Wyatt

A catalogue record of this book
is available from the British Library

ISBN-13 978-0-00-715526-2
ISBN-10 0-00-715526 3

Printed and bound in Great Britain by
Martins the Printers Limited, Berwick upon Tweed

Contents

Introduction   *v*

PART ONE — INSPIRING KIDS' STORIES

1   Discovering Our Shining Potential   3
2   The Journey in Schools   17
3   Partnering Your Child   29
4   Working with Health Concerns   45
5   Issues of Death and Loss   75
6   Using The Journey in Everyday Life   95
7   The Immense Power of Forgiveness   117
8   Divorce and Relationship Issues   129
9   Empowering Internal Resources   145
10   And the Greatest of These is Love …   157

PART TWO — A HEALING ADVENTURE FOR KIDS

11   A Healing Adventure for Kids: Instructions   165
12   A Healing Adventure for Kids   171

PART THREE — THE KIDS' JOURNEY PROCESS FOR
EIGHT TO TWELVE YEAR OLDS

13   The Kids' Journey: Instructions   207
14   The Kids' Journey Process   215
15   Working with Teenagers   231

Gratitude   *235*
Author's Note   *241*

Introduction

This is a book about liberation – about freeing the boundless potential that is shining inside each and every human heart.

Deep inside all of us is a boundless joy, a potential for true genius, an infinite love, a wellspring of creativity. It's waiting there, beckoning, calling you right now, inviting you to discover your own magnificence, urging you to plummet the depths of the wisdom within to discover a vast potential that is capable of creating *anything*.

Each of our children is born *as* this radiant presence, *as* this boundless potential. Unfortunately, through the course of life's pains and trials, their innate radiance may seem to get covered over – with layers of unresolved hurt, moments of failure, emotional shutdowns. It's as if we come in as a brilliant, shining light and somehow life conspires to put a lampshade over it, obscuring it. In time we start to identify with all the layers, forgetting that there ever was a greatness within.

In this book you'll learn very real and practical ways to take that lampshade off. You'll learn simple but powerful tools for liberating that shining magnificence.

This book is full of joy, full of inspiring stories that will speak directly to your own deepest knowing. It is full of real-life accounts of everyday children who have gone on Journeys, freed themselves and taken the lid off their creativity. As we travel with them, we learn how they've healed their bodies and we share their love of life as they peel away the layers and unearth their own genius. We feel the poignancy of their easy ability to forgive that which might seem to be impossible to forgive and, through their Journeys, we see ourselves, and *we* are liberated.

The truth of the children's wisdom, the health and vitality they experience and the simplicity of their awakening serve as a model of possibility to us all, inspiring us and giving us the courage to begin our own Journeys.

This book is also chock-full of practical tools, simple step-by-step process work, everyday wisdom and user-friendly skills, written in what I hope is a down-to-earth style that will encourage you to begin working/playing easily and effectively with your children, starting now.

It is my deepest prayer that, as parents and guardians of these beautiful souls, we truly learn to *partner* our children in their spiritual and healing Journeys. I pray that we recognize that our children are, in fact, already free, whole and full of shining potential.

All that we are doing as partners is helping them to clear away the veils that have obscured that potential, liberating their true selves. We are helping them take the lampshades off their *already* shining lights.

Currently, the Kids' Journey is being used all over the world by schoolteachers, school counsellors and children's therapists. It is being used in addiction treatment centres, by abuse groups, children's support organizations and social services organizations. It has been adopted and used by priests, nuns, ministers, rabbis, monks, pastors and swamis from a wide range of spiritual traditions. Most of all, it is being used by everyday mums, dads, aunts, uncles, grandmothers and grandfathers from all walks of life – people like you and me.

Because there are literally thousands of inspiring kids' stories to choose from, I have included those that deal with everyday issues – the questions and challenges that beset normal children from all cultures. Each story provides us with a lesson on how to address those issues, and specific tools and process work that are designed to liberate and heal the issue. So it's the children themselves who are actually providing us with the teaching we need to lovingly partner them in their healing and growth. I've changed almost all the names, as I feel children deserve the same respect and privacy that we, as adults, feel we need. In some cases I've expanded on the process work to give a fuller explanation and understanding of how it works, but in all cases the actual issues and their moving and extraordinary results are intact, chronicling the children's triumph, awakening and healing.

To make the work easier and more user-friendly, I've organized the book into three main sections:

1. The first section is an introduction to the work. It includes the children's stories, their issues and how they resolved them, ultimately teaching us how to liberate our own shining potential.

2. The second section focuses primarily on our little ones – five to seven year olds. It includes in-depth instructions and then a specially designed therapeutic fairytale-like story that works at a subliminal level with the youngsters. It is like a spiritual adventure and can be read as a bedtime story. Kids love it! Even if you intend working only with older children, I strongly recommend you read this section in full, as it contains many of the teachings on which the older kids' work is predicated.

3. Section three is primarily for working with older kids – eight to twelve year olds – and also has some instructions for working with teenagers. It includes the actual Kids' Journey process together with in-depth instructions.

Finally, if your children inspire you to go on your own Journey, which undoubtedly they will, I recommend you read the original book for adults: *The Journey: An Extraordinary Guide for Healing Your Life and Setting Yourself Free.*

Journeywork was originally born from my own direct experience of healing from a large tumour without drugs or surgery in just six-and-a-half weeks' time. In 1992 I was diagnosed with a large tumour in my uterus. Having served for 15 years in the natural health field as both a teacher/seminar leader and therapist, it was the last thing I had ever expected to take place. I thought I had been doing everything 'right'. I'd attended countless seminars, therapy sessions and had done a huge amount of emotional / physical clearing work – I'd definitely dropped a lot of my emotional 'baggage'. Physically, I lived all the principles I believed in: I meditated daily, did daily exercise, ate clean, vibrant, whole, organic vegetarian food, drank pure filtered water and received regular massage and bodywork. More important than all these things, I felt fulfilled and at peace in my life: I was deeply in love with my husband of 18 years, the kids had been brought up with what I trusted were wholesome and empowering belief systems, and my work was hugely uplifting and satisfying – I travelled worldwide teaching tens of thousands of people how to create vibrant health. I was a living example of all that I believed in: I looked vibrant and healthy, and felt that way inside and out. So the last thing I ever expected was to be diagnosed with a large tumour.

I was sent reeling and was catapulted on a profound healing journey that ultimately led me to face an emotional issue that had remained blocked, stored in my body for years. In freeing that old cell memory, my body was finally able to go about its own natural process of healing.

The Journey was born from my deep desire to share with humanity what Grace had so generously blessed me with: the means to get direct access to our souls, to uncover old repressed cell memories, to release the stored emotions and finally to forgive and complete with these issues so that our bodies and our beings can go about the process of healing naturally.

In the original *Journey* book you join me on my personal healing journey. You are guided step-by-step through the two mind–body healing processes which were born from that experience: the Emotional Journey and the Physical Journey. And you are freshly inspired as you read how others have found true freedom and healing in their own process work.

From the moment *The Journey* was published the work caught fire internationally. Currently hundreds of thousands of people worldwide have read the book, and more importantly are using the process work successfully and fruitfully in their lives. With the Emotional Journey people have successfully cleared issues of grief, loss, abandonment, depression, jealousy, betrayal, low self-esteem, sexual blocks, fear and anxiety. They've cleared chronic fatigue, fear of criticism, long-held guilt, issues of abuse, hostility and rage. With the Physical Journey people have naturally healed from a variety of health concerns, including allergies, acute asthma, eczema, cancer of many kinds, Crohn's disease, tumours, fibroids, sports injuries, arthritis, migraines and even the common cold.

It has been deeply moving to know that so many thousands from all walks of life have successfully participated in their own healing journeys. And it's been equally rewarding to see so many therapeutic and medical practitioners offer Journeywork alongside their own healing work. Cancer centres, orthodox hospitals, alternative health practices, doctors, nurses, homoeopaths, herbalists, kinesiologists, chiropractors, physiotherapists, massage therapists, nutritionists, psychiatrists, psychoanalysts – people in nearly every field of healing, both emotional and physical, have felt free to incorporate Journeywork into their own specialist areas.

This book gives you new, fresh ways of using Journeywork with kids. It's your invitation to partner your child in liberating their shining potential, and I pray it will also be a catalyst for you to begin your own healing journey.

It's time we *all* took the lampshades off our lights.

PART
ONE

Inspiring Kids' Stories

Discovering Our Shining Potential

I recently received a heart-rending letter from a deeply concerned mother of an eight-year-old boy, Matthew. Carla wrote that the school board had come to her about her son. He wasn't keeping up with other students in his class. He couldn't focus or pay attention, and often he appeared withdrawn from the other kids. He'd been diagnosed with Attention Deficit Disorder (ADD) and dyslexia, and his teacher was apologetic and regretful, but she believed Matthew was too dysfunctional to continue at normal primary school. He needed to go to a school for children with learning disorders, as he was beginning to hold back the rest of his class.

Carla was stunned, horrified that they considered her son not only incapable of functioning in a normal school but so disabled that he needed to go to a special school. She just couldn't and wouldn't believe that her son was 'stupid' or abnormal. There must be some mistake, some explanation. She pleaded with the school board and begged that Matthew be allowed to stay at school just one more term. She promised to get him daily tutoring after school and, being a physical therapist herself, she would do regular therapy with her son. She'd also look into getting other alternative therapies that might help.

Reluctantly, the school board agreed, but with the proviso that if Matthew's grades did not improve significantly by the end of term then, regrettably, they would be compelled to let him go and would recommend alternative schools which might be more suitable for him.

Carla gave Matthew her all. In addition to daily tutoring following school, she tried other therapies, including her own field, kinesiology. Matthew's grades began to improve marginally … but not enough. Carla became desperate to reach her son, to find out what was really going on. She just knew in her bones that he was a beautiful and intelligent soul. He had always been a bright child. Even though he had been diagnosed with dyslexia, it did not mean that Matthew was inherently stupid. She just knew that there *must* be some emotional blockage that was holding him back. He was full of potential – she'd seen it from the time he was a toddler; sometimes that potential, that brilliance, would come out at the most unexpected moments. Yet she'd also sensed that there was something holding him back. She had noticed that often Matthew seemed quiet and isolated, shut down and emotionally unavailable. She just didn't know how to get through to him, but with all her being she wanted to help him take this lampshade off his light. She was determined to do whatever it took to help her son find himself, to liberate his true nature, so that he could shine again.

Carla began to pray fervently to find a way to get through to her son. It was at this time that, by chance, she came across *The Journey*. She read the book from cover to cover – she could not put it down. It spoke deeply to her own wisdom. It detailed simple and powerful processes for opening into our true potential, and gave down-to-earth step-by-step tools for clearing emotional and physical blocks that might be obscuring that natural potential. In her heart of hearts Carla knew that Matthew could benefit from the work, if he was willing to participate. And she was thrilled when she turned to the back of the book to find in-depth instructions on how to work with children. She thought, 'What have I got to lose? It's worth asking Matthew if he'd be willing to give it a try.'

Carla briefly explained to Matthew that the Kids' Journey is like a magical fairytale or inner adventure that carries you inside your body to emotional blocks that are stored there. She explained that it would be gentle and healing, and asked if he'd like to give it a go. Matthew shrugged his shoulders. 'Sure, why not?' He wanted to please his mum, and perhaps secretly he hoped it might help. And so Carla turned to the back of the book and began to read the process outlined. Part of the process involves getting access to specific 'cell memories' – limiting patterns which get stored in our cells. For Matthew, The Journey was surprisingly simple. He had no problems focusing or paying attention, because it was like listening to an exciting adventure or a really good bedtime story. *Everyone* likes a good story, especially kids.

Matthew's own inner wisdom seemed to guide him perfectly to the exact place where his emotional block was stored. It guided him to the specific cell memory of when the initial 'shut down' had occurred – when he was only five years old and had just begun to learn his ABCs. In his memory Matthew was newly at school, and what neither his mum nor his schoolteacher knew was that he had an acute problem with his eyesight. He couldn't see things clearly up close. Ever since he was a young child, when something was put directly in front of his eyes it would go all blurry and out of focus. He never told his mum because he thought it was normal, that it was just the way things were. He had no idea that others could see close things with crystal clarity, and it hadn't really been a problem until he started school and was required to write his first letters on a page.

Matthew desperately needed glasses, but no one knew: not his mum, not his teacher, not even Matthew himself.

Matthew kept trying to write the letter 'A', but couldn't figure out why it seemed to come out all wrong on the paper. Across the room, a friend of his held up his paper – his letter 'A' looked perfect, just like the one on the blackboard, but when the teacher came around to check on Matthew's writing, she kept chastising him, telling him to do it better, more accurately, more carefully.

On the third day of learning ABCs the teacher, who was new to the kids and serving as a substitute, grew frustrated with Matthew. Why wasn't he even trying? All the other children could write the letter 'A'. In her frustration, she grabbed his paper out of his hand and marched him to the front of the classroom. Holding up his paper so all the other kids could see, she exclaimed, 'Look at this page. Matthew is so stupid he can't even write the letter "A".' All the kids laughed, and for Matthew time stopped. He froze. He looked into all his friends' faces, laughing and ridiculing him, and the humiliation burned. His face got hot, his stomach began to churn; he couldn't bear it another second. Something inside him shut down. A wall came down: he shut everyone out. The laughter faded into the background, everyone became a blur and he turned his face away and ran out of the room.

That afternoon when his mum picked him up from school he was unusually quiet, and when she asked him, 'How was school today?', all he could reply was, 'OK.' He felt too ashamed to tell her what had happened. Everyone thought he was stupid. Everyone who mattered had laughed. And now he felt numb to it all, incapable of finding his way through it. A wall had come down internally. He found himself shut down and shut out.

After that he could no longer focus at school. He didn't care what the teacher said and didn't want to hear. It didn't matter anyway – he was stupid, so why bother?

Three months later, it was finally discovered that Matthew needed glasses, but by that time the damage had already been done and there would never be any way for Matthew to truly connect with and be part of school fun and learning in a healthy way again … not until he did his first Journey process.

Like Matthew most of us have had childhood experiences where we have felt unable to cope. I'm sure you can imagine how easy it would be to shut down in the face of such humiliation. Matthew's story could be any of our stories. Maybe for you it wasn't a paper being held up in front of the class; maybe it was being ridiculed in the playground or not making the sports team. None of us were trained in how to deal with these issues, and so often we found ourselves withdrawing or pretending it didn't matter, losing ourselves in our colouring books or refusing to play with the other kids, all the while feeling desperately alone, alienated, excluded and not knowing a way out of our own pain or a way into the 'in' crowd.

During Matthew's Journey process, not only did he access this old memory but he finally faced, released and let go of all the pain of the humiliation that he had carried for so long. He came to realize that his teacher didn't really think he was stupid; she was just frustrated. She didn't know he needed glasses; she just thought he wasn't trying hard enough. Now that he had finally felt and expressed all of his stored shame and hurt, he found he was able to forgive easily. His mother did the 'Change Memory' process with him, where in his mind's eye Matthew revisited the old memory, played it out on a video screen and then played it out a second time, but now seeing how it *would* have been if he'd had access to a whole host of more supportive and healthy emotional resources at that time. (More on this in Chapter 9.) He received a lot of imaginary balloons which gave him the internal emotional resources he *would* have needed at the time of the humiliation. His mother gave him a balloon of self-confidence which he breathed in until it filled his whole body. Then she gave him a whole series of balloons: courage, a sense of humour, the knowledge that the teacher was just frustrated, the knowledge that his friends all loved him and that they were only laughing because the teacher had made fun of him. He received balloons of self-worth, self-love and the ability to understand what was taking place. He also got a crystal dome balloon that allowed him to be inside a protected space, so any ridicule would roll off of him and he could just be at peace inside. Finally, he got a balloon of innate intelligence and the ability to reach out to his friends. He breathed in all of these beautiful qualities.

When he played the memory again, this time with all his balloons, he was able to see how it *would* have gone if he had had all those internal resources at that time. He found he was still hauled to the front of the class, but when the teacher criticized his paper it just rolled off him – he realized his teacher was just in a bad mood and frustrated; she didn't know he needed glasses. When he looked into the faces of the other children he saw that they were laughing *with* him, not *at* him, and he himself broke into peals of laughter – laughing at his own paper, saying what a mess it was – and later he joked easily with the other kids as they played together.

Matthew realized in his Journey process that the teacher just didn't understand that he needed glasses – neither had *he* at the time. Realizing that it didn't matter anyway because all his friends liked him, glasses or no glasses, he forgave his teacher and the kids. When his Journey was over (after about 20 minutes) he opened his eyes and looked at his mum with a clarity that he hadn't had in ages.

The Friday after his first Journey process he got his first 'A' and over the next several months became the brightest student in his class.

Carla was overwhelmed with joy when she wrote to tell me that Matthew was performing healthily at school – no more Attention Deficit Disorder, no more dyslexia.

So often we seem to label our children, giving them labels for behaviour we don't understand. We pigeonhole them into a dysfunctional syndrome and see them through the filter of that syndrome, forgetting the beautiful, radiant souls that they really are. These days it has become almost fashionable to label kids and then put them on drugs – as if narcotizing them could possibly get to the root cause of their problem. It really is a crime, and very sad indeed that in our ignorance of how to cope with behaviour we can't understand why we try to put that behaviour to sleep with drugs, mood-altering chemicals that change the very character and personality of these innocent souls, when all that is really needed is to uncover an emotional block and buried emotion that is part of what co-created these supposed 'syndromes' in the first place.

Matthew's story could be your story; it could be mine. Recently I was in South Africa where The Journey is being used by teachers in primary schools. After I gave a school assembly programme to 800 shining, beaming children, I walked out into the school car park. There, two parents were standing in their Sunday best clothes, clearly having taken time off work to meet me personally. They stood there patiently waiting in the hot African sun with their three beautiful children, all in starched white shirts and school uniforms.

When I approached the mother, she had tears in her eyes. She simply said, 'Thank you for giving me my son Daniel back... He'd been so withdrawn and aggressive towards his brothers and sister and had become so anti-social we didn't know what to do with him. He was failing at school. Our doctor said he had ADD and put him on Ritalin, and his behaviour had become a little better. But I hadn't really *seen* my son in three years. Do you know what I mean? It was as though he was under a dark cloud and I couldn't reach him. But after Jayshree, his teacher, worked with him with The Journey – she did four processes with him – he became so joyous and loving towards his brothers and sister that we took him off the drugs. Now he's thriving at school and playing with the other kids in the playground. Recently he won an academic award for excellence in *all* his subjects! Thank you, thank you, thank you for giving us our son back. That's all we wanted to say to you – thank you.'

I was overwhelmed. I simply looked into her son's eyes and said, 'He shines like a diamond! What a beautiful being. Jayshree is an amazing teacher – she really cares about her students. She genuinely wants to bring out the best in them. I'm so glad your son opened up and let her in. And thank God he let *himself* out.'

Later, Jayshree shared with me that when she was teaching a class about geography and gold mining, she asked the kids, 'Where do you think we find gold?' No one raised their hand. Then Daniel jumped to his feet, hand in the air, and said, 'I know!'

'So, Daniel, where do you find gold?' Jayshree asked.

'In your heart, ma'am. That's where the real gold is,' he replied.

Jayshree was blown away by the answer. The simple, innocent wisdom of children can, indeed, take our breath away.

Here is an excerpt from the letter Daniel's mother subsequently sent to me:

> ... *My only hope was that he would take the medication, which controlled his attention in class so he could at least finish some work and barely pass. The medication helped him to keep focused and not daze off into his own world. He also managed to write in a straight line when on medication. However, he became very quiet, withdrawn and silent. He never laughed or played like the other kids and always looked so serious.*

Then his teacher suggested that he try something new called The Journey, which had helped her family. And I thought that no harm could be done, so let's give it a small try. She worked with him in the class and then at her home for ten minutes at a time. She also gave him special notes of motivation and encouragement, which he read all the time and kept in his top pocket. Two weeks later, I took my boy off the medication! He was answering questions in class, participating in sports, laughing, running — he was a normal child again!

Because The Journey is so widely used in so many countries, I hear these kinds of stories every week. Yet they never cease to awe me. The courage of the human soul, and the ability of the body and being to heal, no matter what our age, is astonishing.

2

The Journey in Schools

All of us come into this world as this same vast potential, yet so often life can seem to conspire to cover that natural radiance, obscure our genius, shut down our joy, block out the love. Still we sense that just beneath the surface there lies true greatness – if only we could get access to it. The Journey gives us the tools – simple step-by-step processes – for finally liberating that shining potential, so it can be fully expressed, wholesomely and joyously, in our lives.

In South Africa, at the school where I gave the assembly programme for 800 beaming school kids, I spoke of this very phenomenon in a general metaphor that I felt both kids and adults could relate to. I said that we all come into this world as a big bright shining diamond, completely whole, radiant and pure. We come in as a vast presence of love and joy, as a huge open potential that is capable of creating anything. And then, through the traumas of life, this diamond can seem to get covered over with layer upon layer of limiting patterns – the time we failed our exam at school; the time our brother or sister made fun of us in front of our playmates; the time we got shy and said all the wrong things to our first crush and they were off-hand with us. As we got older it could be the time we were interviewed for our first job and were so awkward and silly that we blew it, and later still it could be the time when we were at work and made a bad mistake then tried to pretend it didn't happen or, even worse, let someone else take the blame … Layer upon layer upon layer our shining radiance gets covered over, until sometimes, as adults, we forget that there ever was a brilliant diamond inside. Instead, we identify with all the mess, the layers that cover it.

I told the kids that this was, in fact, exactly what had happened to me. As an adult, I completely forgot that there was a beautiful diamond inside. Instead, I identified with all the layers that covered it … until one day I got very sick. And part of the great blessing of my healing journey was that it carried me deep inside, where I uncovered a shining radiance that I realized had been there all along. I fell so in love with this light that I didn't want *anything* to cover it anymore and so I began a process of clearing out all the layers that had previously hidden it. In that process, not only did my body heal, but I felt as though the *real* me had finally been set free. I'd finally taken the lampshade off my light.

I then asked, 'How many of you are already aware of this light shining deep within you?' Eight hundred hands shot up all at once – some kids practically stood up, their hands went up so fast. Then I asked, 'Would you like to go on a magical Journey right into the core of this light – right into your very own diamond?'

'YES, MA'AM!' resounded 800 bell-like voices in a huge cacophony of sound so loud it felt like it shook the rafters. It was so loud that everyone burst into laughter. I then asked, *'So are you ready to start?'*

'YES, MA'AM!' followed by more laughter so loud that one kid actually fell off his seat, which of course produced even more laughter.

After it all died down, conspiratorially I said, 'Well, I need your help, though. In order to go on this inner adventure, you will really need to pay full attention and go for it – otherwise the headmistress may get mad at me!' I winked in her direction. 'Do you all promise to pay extra close attention and go for it, so I won't get in trouble?'

'YES, MA'AM!' came the enthusiastic reply, as some of the kids glanced in the headmistress's direction, just to see if she approved.

Once we'd all settled down we began with the first ever simultaneous live Journey process with 800 joyous and enthusiastic souls aged five to eleven. And what a magical time we had. The little ones sometimes had a bit of trouble keeping their eyes closed, and kept peeking to see if everyone else was doing it right, but on the whole, I could tell it was all going very well. Even though their eyes were closed, their faces were so animated, they clearly were following the directions with gusto. Some of the kids were gesticulating with their hands, as if they were holding real balloons, while others were mouthing their conversations at the 'campfire'. Children are so natural and open. They're already aware of their own inner light, and processing with them is always a joy. By the end, they were all smiling, and everyone seemed to complete successfully.

Ten minutes after we'd begun, everyone opened their eyes and they were just *beaming*! They looked so beautiful and shiny that spontaneously I said, 'Why don't you look straight into the eyes of the person next to you and say, "You are such a beautiful person. I love the light I see in your eyes!"' Many of them giggled when they spoke the words, but they all did so.

By now the room was full of laughter, but as I watched I realized that for many of these kids this was the very first time anyone had actually uttered those words to them, and many were quietly and secretly moved as they deeply drank in the words.

When the assembly was over, a rush of 800 kids wanting hugs and autographs came flooding. I was swamped from all sides! A huge hugging fest went on for about an hour and a quarter, with all our Journey staff joining in, signing autographs and receiving hugs. Sometimes the individual queues were over 200 children long, all politely waiting their turn. Each one wanted a special message whispered into their ear and then they'd run to the corners of the room to share what had been said with all their classmates. It was a pure celebration of joy.

Eventually the headmistress, who had been more than patient, insisted that everyone go back to their respective classrooms. For a moment it seemed as if we were resting in a soft lull, but then, quietly and secretly, one by one, the *teachers* came sneaking out of their classrooms, offering their gratitude and giving huge warm hugs. Then the headmistress put her foot down once and for all, and teachers and students alike returned to their classrooms.

Finally I was allowed to meet privately with the class of children who had been using Journeywork regularly over the past year. I was already aware that their teacher, Jayshree Mannie, and two other teachers had done a year of case studies, dividing the kids into three groups: one group received no Journeywork; one group only occasional Journeywork and one group received Journeywork every Friday afternoon. At the end of the year they tallied the results – and the statistics were extraordinary! The students who got no Journeywork averaged a 67 per cent pass rate. Those who received only occasional Journeywork averaged a 76 per cent pass rate. Those who did Journeywork every week averaged a whopping 91 to 93 per cent!

I was curious to find out what had taken place with the children *personally*, not just academically, so I sat with them and asked what they had discovered inside themselves. One child said that she'd found love inside and that she was nicer to her brothers and sisters, another said he'd found courage and understanding and that his grades had improved. Another said she could actually see the 'love-light', as she called it, in other kids. When she said this I asked them all, 'Now that you've uncovered this love, this light inside, will you promise to help the other kids take the lampshades off their lights? Will you help them discover their courage, their understanding, their fun, their wisdom?' Everyone promised wholeheartedly to become a torch to help light the other kids' lamps.

I had already received several beautiful letters from the parents of this class about how their children were much more open, loving and socially well-adjusted, and kinder to their siblings; and they were thrilled with the academic results. I also received dozens of letters from the kids, but it was somehow more meaningful to hear it from the kids first hand and to see it shining in their eyes.

Here are a couple of parents' letters I received, which I thought you might find inspiring:

> *My son was underachieving at school and was not performing well in his karate class. I had attended a Journey workshop and saw the merits of The Journey and tried this on Winston myself. However, I think that being his mother did not help too much, so I took him to Jayshree for a Journey session which lasted 35 minutes.*
>
> *Two days later he was fine. He excelled at his karate championship and won a medal! Better still, I received a concerned call from the school and I frantically rushed there. The teachers said that they were baffled by Winston's results ... They had marked and remarked and remarked his scripts because his marks had improved by 65 per cent, and he was now topping the class! Before he was at the bottom end! They could not understand this and neither would I explain! I felt that it was a private issue and preferred not to say any more!*

Winston is Head Boy now and we are all proud. I am doing Journeywork privately and can honestly swear by its success!

We had been beset with tragedies in our family, losing six members to cancer. Our daughter Tanya was suffering as we had just lost another favourite aunt. She was doing badly at school, was not sleeping well, had nightmares and was not eating properly. My sister told me about the Journey as she had brought her kids along. I saw the difference in her kids and decided to give it a shot.

One session later and Tanya was changed! Her chronic earache was gone! She was eating and putting on weight nicely and was sleeping well. Her grades were coming along nicely too. She did discuss that her fear of death was so strong that she had decided that it was not safe to enjoy life as we all would die soon anyway. And all this was because of the tragedies. She internalized this fear and literally stopped living!

Thanks to The Journey, she is a normal happy kid again!

Jayshree Mannie is continuing to take Journeywork to children all over South Africa, only now she is reaching into ghettos, working with social programmes like Life Line, molestation groups and abuse centres, and she's teaching other schoolteachers, so that they can reach out to children to help them all liberate their shining potential.

We are all kids. Our bodies and our beings so want us to heal. When we take but one step towards Grace, it takes a thousand steps towards us.

3

Partnering Your Child

For us to work with children, the work must first start with us. We must see our children as *already* whole, free, inherently wise and beautiful. Then, when we partner them in their personal and spiritual journeys, all that we are really doing is helping to lift off the layers of imposed limitations – the lies, the hurt, the emotional blocks that obscure their natural potential. That potential is already here, already free – all that we are doing is liberating it, allowing it to be expressed wholesomely and joyously.

So often parents come to me and say that they really don't know how to 'get through' to their kids; they seem so emotionally inexpressive. Isn't it true? When your child comes home from school and you ask, 'So how was school today?' what does your child inevitably answer? Usually it's 'OK' or 'Fine', nothing more, nothing less. No one gave these kids (or any of us for that matter) the manual 'How to Feel and Express your Emotions', and so generally the most common response from kids of all ages is a shrugging of the shoulders and a one-word reply that doesn't tell us anything. Have you ever found yourself quietly frustrated because you're not even sure which questions to ask anymore? And have you ever had the sense that something more might be going on, but you can't quite put your finger on it? I'm sure that every parent out there has experienced this frustration.

My husband Kevin and I had first-hand experience of this a few years ago. Kevin's son Mark is a beautiful, angelic, highly intelligent 11 year old. He's always been bright, quick to fall in with his peers, compassionate to younger kids and socially well-adjusted. He's well-liked by teachers and pupils alike, and always brings home stellar school reports. When he was eight years old, we began to notice that when we brought up the subject of theme parks, his response was always lacklustre. As he was not an overly emotive child, his response wasn't terribly concerning, but nonetheless, when you suggest going to Disneyland or Universal Studios to kids you can usually expect an excited or effusive response. Mark's was almost always one of indifference. It seemed odd, but how do you penetrate that kind of malaise? We never knew what was behind his quietness until Mark attended the Junior Journey for the first time and underwent his first Kids' Journey.

The Junior Journey is a fun-filled empowering programme for children aged eight to eleven. The one-day workshop is jam-packed with confidence- and self-esteem building exercises, and each child receives a private Kids' Journey with a Journey Accredited Therapist (we have one therapist there for every two kids). They have guided 'Sleeping Elephant' meditation, they paint 'before' and 'after' pictures of their Journeywork, and they have a real-life bonfire where they throw in all the old unresourceful patterns or behaviour that held them back in the past – and they usually also roast marshmallows. They playact scenes using their resource balloons (something you'll learn more about later), and they end the day with a self-esteem and confidence-building game – when the ball is thrown to you, you have to go into the middle of the circle and one by one each child shares what they like best about you.

The responses we get from both kids and parents are just phenomenal. Usually kids have massive positive shifts and the parents are just thrilled with the results.

Mark was attending the programme for the first time and usually we suggest that kids get their first few Journeys with someone other than their parents, as it gives the child the same privacy and anonymity that we, as adults, often feel we need. So Mark was to undergo his first Kids' Journey with one of the Accredited Therapists at the programme.

As expected, Mark threw himself into the day (most kids do, it's so much fun!) and fell in easily with the other kids. When it came time for his process, Sally, the head therapist, decided that she would work with him in his private session.

During his Journey, Mark went back to a memory of when he was seven years old. We had taken him to Legoland and had encouraged him to go on the little 'Dragon' roller-coaster. All of Legoland is pretty much aimed at younger kids, so when Mark seemed reluctant to go on the 'Dragon' with us, Kevin softly encouraged him, reassuring him that it would be fun. Mark begrudgingly acquiesced and we all three got on the ride together. Mark seemed to be enjoying himself until we got to the last hill of the ride. We could feel the roller-coaster slowly cranking up the hill and as I looked up at the steepness, even I thought, 'Hmm, this is a bit high for little kids,' but as there was nothing we could do, we just laughed and held Mark closer to us. As we went roaring down the other side of the hill, Mark turned white and looked as though he was either going to laugh or cry – we couldn't tell which. Kevin, cognisant of Mark's nervousness, tried to encourage him, and as we got off the ride softly reassured him, affirming how brave Mark was and how much fun the ride had been.

What neither of us had realized at the time was that Mark had been terrified, and he was secretly furious that we hadn't listened to him in the first place.

During his Kids' Journey, at his 'campfire', he finally got to let loose at us, and he released all of the stored-up anger and forgave us for not listening. When he had finished, he spoke to Sally, who then came to us on his behalf to say that Mark really wanted to make his own decisions about roller-coasters and felt that we needed to listen to him more.

Whoa, were we surprised ... but also grateful. We had no idea it had affected him so strongly. It seemed like such a harmless thing – a three-minute ride on a kiddie roller-coaster. And yet it was pointing to something much larger: that we really needed to listen more deeply to Mark, to hear his needs and respond to them more respectfully.

Later, when Kevin spoke with Mark privately, he let him know how sorry we were and that neither of us had realized how scared he had been – that his lack of communication *prior* to the ride had left us in the dark as to what his true feelings were. Kevin asked Mark to promise him that if ever he felt afraid he would let us know. Mark admitted that he was shy and a little scared of telling us, but he promised in future to listen more carefully to himself and his body, and if he felt any fear at all he'd let us know. Kevin promised in return that we would never make him do anything he was too scared to do. He reassured him that we would never take him anywhere where there was real danger, that we love him too much and that if he was frightened we wouldn't force him into anything he genuinely didn't want to do. Kevin also agreed he would endeavour to listen more closely, more deeply, and got Mark to agree that communication is a two-way street – though a great deal can be conjectured and surmised, you can't assume you can mind read just from someone's body language, you need to verbalize your feelings.

Since that time, it has been ongoing learning. To strengthen Mark, we still like to encourage him to meet his fears and stretch to take action, even when fear is coming up. But he's never since been made to do something that he really hasn't chosen to do himself.

Now, whenever we go to Universal Studios or Disney, Mark chooses which rides he wants to take. Last summer at Universal Studios we went on the dread 'Jurassic Park' ride, the scariest of all the water-splash roller-coaster rides, and Mark asked to ride it three times! It was his favourite ride in the whole theme park. But more important, we as parents are learning to *partner* Mark on his journey, rather than foisting our ideas of what's best for him onto him without his input. We are all learning how to listen and how to express ourselves clearly.

Part of what you will be doing as you work with your child is learning just this: how to *partner* your child in opening into their own experience, and how to support them in discovering their own truth and their own answers – a lesson that would be good for all of us to learn in *all* our relationships!

Recently I shared Mark's story with one of our senior Accredited Therapists, Gaby, who had served as a trainer two years ago at a Junior Journey programme. She remarked that it reminded her of a process she'd had with a child who had seemed quite quiet and shy. Gerald seemed to like keeping himself to himself, which is unusual in the normally social and interactive kids' programme. His aloneness touched Gaby and she felt in her heart that she would be the right trainer to do his process with him.

Respecting Gerald's natural quietness, Gaby began the process with a tender sensitivity and lightness. In the Kids' Journey the child imagines going down a set of ten steps, knowing that every step they take will carry them into a place of safety and relaxation and that on the bottom step they will open into an ocean of light, a vast presence of peace and love. Gerald took to the process easily, loved opening into the peace and love, and when he was on the bottom step described to Gaby that, in his mind's eye, he was sitting by himself on a warm beach, happy and alone, basking in the sun. Gaby noted that he said he was alone and asked if he felt alright in his aloneness. 'Oh, yes, I'm very happy. I like to be alone.' It seemed clear that he was genuinely content, so Gaby continued with the process.

In his mind's eye Gerald walked through the door, greeted his mentor and together they stepped into an imaginary space shuttle – so magical that it can carry you safely and gracefully into any part of the body. It carries you to the specific place where an emotional issue is stored. Gerald loved 'cruising' in the space shuttle and it guided him very easily and naturally to a part of his body where a specific cell memory was stored. Surprisingly, the memory had almost the opposite feeling to the beach scene. Apparently, when he was about three-and-a-half years old his parents had taken him to a firework display on a warm summer's night. Everyone screamed and 'oohed' and 'aahed' as the explosions in the sky blasted one after the other, but Gerald kept telling his parents that he didn't feel comfortable and he didn't want to be there. Sitting in the dark, not knowing what was coming next, then the blinding light followed by huge thunderous explosions, the screams of excitement coming from everywhere, from faces he couldn't even see – it was all too much for him. All he craved was a nice warm quiet place where he could just rest peacefully. He tried to express himself, but the more he spoke up, the more his parents 'shushed' him, overriding his discomfort and softly coaxing him not to be a baby – 'Everyone else is enjoying it.'

To many of us, this may seem like a harmless enough memory. Haven't we all been 'shushed' at some time or another? Haven't we all been told in some way or other that 'children should be seen and not heard'? And yet what made this particular memory so potent was that Gerald was extremely scared; he was in a *peak emotional state*. Repeatedly the loud noises and screams frightened him anew and yet he was basically told to 'stuff it'. So he shut down internally. His body got the message: 'If I feel a strong emotion and express it, I'll just be made to shut up.' From that he construed: 'It's not OK to feel those feelings and it's certainly not OK to express them.' In that realization, something happened inside Gerald: 'If I'm not allowed to feel or express my feelings, then I'd rather be alone. That way I won't have anyone around me to stir up scary or intense emotions, and I can feel safe just to be myself.' At three and a half he'd already experienced the crystallizing event that would change the whole way he viewed the world, and indeed change his personality. In that moment a loner was born.

So often we wonder what makes one child so outgoing and another so tentative and retiring. Often mothers and fathers will say innocently, 'Well, she's been like that since she was a toddler – it's just her personality.' Yet that crystallizing 'shut-down' can have such a profound effect that often as adults we enter into intimate relationships and wonder why we just can't feel the connection or the closeness. Somehow we can feel love in our own hearts for the other person, but their love doesn't seem to penetrate into the deepest part of us. Often, we'll go to parties and wonder, 'Why is it that in the midst of this crowd, I feel alone? I know everyone, we all get on, everyone is friendly and caring, and yet I feel like an outsider.' Well, that pattern may have started with an early childhood shut-down just like Gerald's.

Perhaps you are already aware of the extraordinary research that has recently been published in the field of cellular biology. Dr Candace Pert, author of the bestselling book *Molecules of Emotion*, is a well-known cellular biologist who works in Washington, DC. On a number of occasions she has spoken to the US Congress about her amazing findings on the effect that *repressed emotions* have on our cells. What she has unequivocally discovered is that whenever we have an intense, powerful emotion that we repress or shut down, specific chemical changes take place in our bodies. These can affect certain cell receptors, blocking those cells from communicating with the other cells in our bodies. If these affected cells remain blocked over a long period of time then there is an increased likelihood that if disease occurs, it will occur in the part of the body where the cell receptors are blocked.

Perhaps this may help explain why it is that one seemingly harmless event like Gerald being shushed at the firework display had

such a potent and long-term effect: the cell memory and its programming got passed on from one cell generation to the next. The
actual memory occurred at only three-and-a-half years of age, yet
the pattern and the decision made from that memory were still
running on automatic pilot at eight years of age.

The internalization 'Being around others might make me feel
intense and scary emotions and as I'm not allowed to feel or
express those, I'd rather be alone', that entire consciousness, that
programming, got passed from cell generation to cell generation.

In order to negatively programme our cells, we have to be in a
peak emotional state *and* we have to repress that emotion at the
time. This repressive action is what releases the chemistry that can
begin the programming or blocking process. Gerald had experienced both sides of the equation – he had been in a peak emotional state *and* had repressed his feelings.

What Candace Pert also observed is that when we feel and
express our emotions healthily, fully and wholesomely, our cell
receptors remain open.

What The Journey process does is to guide you in a safe, gentle
and wholesome way to *specific* cell memories, so that you can
finally feel and release the stored pain, let go of the story and

memory and forgive the people involved. Then you are given healthy, empowering internal emotional resources so that you can wholesomely and freely respond to life in the future.

When Gerald finished his process, not only had he finally faced and released all the intense emotion from that memory but he had wholeheartedly forgiven his parents. He also received a whole set of resource balloons which helped give his body and being positive and healthy reprogramming. He was given a balloon that allowed him to feel safe, even when there is loud noise and excitement around him, and another balloon that let him feel safe in a crowd. He received balloons of courage, self-confidence, the ability to play with others, light-heartedness, joy and the ability to feel his emotions, to express himself clearly and to share his feelings at the right time with his parents and peers.

After his process, Gaby noticed that at first Gerald remained on the outskirts of what was happening with the other kids. But slowly and tentatively he began to join in, and by the end of the day he was playing as rambunctiously and noisily as all the other kids. When they all did the 'Monkey Rap' song, where they all mirror each other in monkey gestures to loud and joyous music, Gerald couldn't stop laughing as he pretended to be a mischievous monkey mimicking the movements of an eight-year-old girl.

Previously, Gerald was destined to be a loner. Who knows? Maybe now he will end up being the life and soul of the party, a shining star in his world.

Dear Brandon

My name is Lindsay Wilson. I am turning 13 this year. I am a boy who did the Children's Journey workshop in 2002. I really enjoyed it because, while I was there I got to meet new people; adults and children – people I wouldn't normally meet. All day long we got to play and have fun and games and we got to know everyone and how everyone felt.

I got to do this special Journey, just for me. It was really good, because I got to express a lot of my feelings and work out a lot of my problems with my Dad. Now that I'm working things out with my Dad, we're getting along a lot better.

After the Journey, I felt a lot better and a big weight was taken off my chest and felt free to get on with the rest of my life. HOORAY!

I get on easily with my family and friends now and I'm not so angry anymore. Before, people couldn't touch me or bump into me without me getting angry and hitting them – even if they said they were sorry.

Now, I can stay calm and I am able to walk away from a fight.

Thank you for creating the Journey so other people like me can feel better, relaxed and enjoy life.

I AM SO HAPPY!!!

4

Working with Health Concerns

The Journey is a deeply spiritual and liberating process that helps awaken us to our true potential. It allows our *real* selves, our own inner essence to shine, to be fully experienced, and it clears out emotional issues, negative beliefs, unhealthy vows, limitations of all kinds that have blocked or obscured that natural potential. It is a simple step-by-step process that enables us to clear out the hurt, lies and circumstances that have prevented us from allowing our shining potential to fully express itself.

In a nutshell, The Journey is a tool for liberation, a process for awakening, work that guides you deep into your soul and clears out all the limiting patterns. It opens you into the infinite, the boundless presence of love that is your own shining potential.

And the second aspect of The Journey, for which it is equally well known, possibly even better known, is as a tool for healing.

One of the blessings of my own remarkable healing journey was that I uncovered a means to access repressed cell memories and clear them completely, so that the body and the being could go about the process of healing naturally. So The Journey is not just for emotional and spiritual liberation – one of the powerfully positive side-effects is that it can be physically healing as well.

At that time much of the medical research on cellular healing was already available. Dr Deepak Chopra, a distinguished medical doctor and one of the leaders in the cellular healing field, had done a rare thing. He had decided that he wanted to discover what makes some people heal from serious illness against the odds, without drugs or surgery. He made a career study of the successful survivors of terminal disease to find out the process that made them heal.

After amassing hundreds (eventually thousands) of case studies, he found that he could find only two qualities in common among the survivors: the first was that, through some act of Grace, some spontaneous event or some spiritual revelation, they all got access to the boundless potential inside. The second was that they all got spontaneous access to the cell memories stored in the part of the body where the disease was.

What is known about the cells inside our body is that they replicate at varying speeds. Old cells die and new ones are born at different rates in different parts of the body. For instance, have you ever noticed that it takes about three weeks or so for your suntan to fade? That's because it takes the skin cells roughly three weeks to regenerate. It takes our liver six weeks to renew itself and our stomach lining only about three or four days. The one that seems almost inconceivable is our eyes – we have all-new eyeballs *every two days or less*; that's how long it takes for every cell in the eyes to replicate. This was so hard for my mind to conceive of until my mother went into hospital for eye surgery. They slit open her eye, inserted a lens and put the flap back. Only a day-and-a-half later they removed the protective eye patch and she could see clearly – that's how quickly eye cells replicate. In fact, there is not a single molecule in your body today that was here a year ago – your body is literally all new. It is continuously renewing itself.

Deepak, however, asked a question that no one else was asking at that time: 'If it's true that our cells are constantly renewing themselves, why is it that, for example, a liver that is riddled with cancer in January is still diseased in June? If the cells of the liver are completely new every six weeks, why isn't the liver completely healed?'

What he postulated at the time, and what has subsequently been verified by more current scientific research, is that stored inside the degenerative cells is suppressed cell memory – some unresolved emotional trauma or limiting pattern. Before the degenerative cells die, they pass on their programming, their consciousness, to the next cells being born. So the new cells are created as exact replicas of the old degenerative cells. The cell memory is passed on from one cell generation to the next.

What Deepak discovered in the case of successful survivors of serious illness is that if they opened into the boundless potential, the infinite body wisdom, the awareness that is responsible for making your heart beat and your hair grow, *and* if they got access to the specific cell memory and cleared it out, the programming was interrupted and was *not* passed on to the next cell generation. Fresh, regenerative cells were born devoid of the previous programming, and cellular healing was the result.

I had read all this research and knew absolutely that cellular healing was possible, but up to that point *no one had given us a method!* How do you get access to that infinite potential? And after you've done that, how do you access the right cell memory? You can learn all the science you want, you can listen to all the theories out there, but it's one thing to know and understand a theory and it's quite another to have a practical step-by-step method that works.

I had made an agreement with my surgeon that if, in four weeks' time, the tumour hadn't significantly healed, then I would let her do what she felt was urgently needed – which was to surgically remove it. This, of course, went against everything I believed in and had learned from alternative medicine. I simply had to buy myself some time to see if I could heal naturally.

Well, I was three weeks into my healing journey. Up to that point I'd done everything I knew to help my body heal: I'd taken herbs and homoeopathic remedies; I'd received colonic irrigation and massage every other day; I'd done emotional release work and neuro-linguistic programming (NLP) work; I'd meditated; I'd refined my diet to the most cleansing food intake possible – 100 per cent fresh and raw organic fruit and vegetables with loads of freshly-squeezed juices; I'd taken enzymes and colloidal minerals – I'd done everything! I looked vibrantly healthy, but my tummy was still as hard as a rock, stretched as taut as a drum, and I still looked five months pregnant.

I began to despair that I would never find a way to get access to the cell memory. *I knew for certain* that part of my healing would lay in uncovering that emotional block, yet no one had published a 'how-to' guide.

I was lying on a massage table, still having seen no measurable result, and I felt like a complete failure. I didn't know where to turn, or even what questions to ask anymore. I'd tried everything

I knew in the natural health field and still had not succeeded. I felt deeply sorry for myself and was overcome with hopelessness. I had run out of options. I had no more answers, and something inside me just gave up. All striving finished, I just lay there in complete surrender, in total innocence.

Unexpectedly, I began to feel the room fill with a palpable presence of peace. It was as if I was soaking in a bath of stillness. In that stillness I heard myself spontaneously pray, 'Please, somehow, let me be guided to uncover that cell memory and complete with it. Please let me be guided to heal.' Then, lying there, unmoving, in the pure innocence of not knowing what else to do, spontaneously I *was* guided directly into the tumour.

What I uncovered was an old familiar memory of childhood violence. Immediately my thinking mind checked in and chastised me, saying, 'It can't be *that* memory! You know all about that one – you went through years of therapy clearing that old stuff.' 'Been there, done that, got the T-shirt!' said my *thinking* mind. But it was almost as though my mind was saying, 'You've already handled it,' and my body and soul were saying, 'Well, you may *think* you've handled it, but you clearly haven't.'

So I thought, 'Well, what have I got to lose? Even if it's not the right memory, it can't hurt to go through one more healing process.'

And so, in the way I'd previously learned, I went about the process of facing and clearing the issue. When I had finished, I felt as though I had arrived in the same place that I'd experienced for several years: neutral acceptance. I decided to ask the presence of peace in the room if I was complete, and the simple word 'No' arose.

Once again I was plunged into the depths of despair. I didn't even know if I'd found the right memory, and even if I had, I obviously wasn't complete and had no clue how to complete. In despair, once again something inside me gave up. Once again, I'd run out of answers and didn't know where to turn. Once again, I just surrendered.

As I lay there, I began to feel the room fill with a vast, scintillating presence of peace, and another prayer spontaneously gave birth to itself: 'Please let me complete with this issue – I don't know what else to do.' Again, I just lay there in silence and unknowing, and *again* out of the stillness a simple word arose: 'Forgiveness.' I wondered, 'Could that be a key? It couldn't be that easy, could it? Well, I've got nothing to lose.'

And so I began to forgive. In the forgiveness I realized there is a quantum leap between accepting what has happened to you and truly forgiving it. The letting go into forgiveness was intensely

emotional: I had to let go of my pride, my blame and my indigna-
tion – it ravaged my heart, but gradually my heart began to soften
and release. Finally, I forgave completely. In that moment, I
realized that the tumour had never been clinging to me: *I* had
been clinging to *it*. Thirty years of blame were over. I'd finally
let go of the story.

Over the next three weeks, I did the process twice more. It was still
much the same issue, but it was as if I was cleaning different facets
of the same diamond. And my tummy grew flatter and flatter.

Three-and-a-half weeks later (about the time it takes for uterine
cells to replicate), I went to Cedars Sinai hospital in Los Angeles
and had a whole battery of medical tests done. I had 43 pictures
taken of my uterus and I was pronounced textbook-perfect clean,
tumour-free and completely whole. I felt like the luckiest person
alive.

I was aware that Grace had blessed me not only with my life and
health but also with the guidance to find a way to heal naturally.
I knew in my heart that this gift wasn't meant just for me – it
belonged to everyone, to the whole of humanity – and that part of
the way I could express my gratitude was to pass this knowledge
and teaching on.

Over the next year, I began working with people with all kinds of issues, emotional and physical. People came with rage issues, depression, unremitting grief, low self-esteem, debilitating fear, chronic and acute arthritis, cancer, Crohn's disease, chronic fatigue, skin diseases and many more. Two different processes evolved out of the work: the Emotional Journey, for emotional blocks, and the Physical Journey, for physical issues and cell memory release. I was amazed as people from all walks of life successfully underwent the process of healing. It didn't seem to matter what their background or their age – each one seemed capable of opening into the infinite potential, each one was able to turn on the flashlight inside, and each one was able to discover the root cause of the issue, release it, clear it out and forgive. Then their bodies went about the process of healing quite naturally as a result.

Since that time, over 100,000 people have read *The Journey* and tens of thousands are using Journeywork – doctors, nurses and health practitioners from all fields, both orthodox and alternative, in hospitals, rehabilitation groups, alternative health centres and addiction clinics. It is used alongside chemotherapy in cancer clinics. Homoeopaths use it. Physiotherapists use it. And, of course, it is used by private individuals in their own homes.

People all over the world have participated in their own healing process by using Journeywork or by incorporating it into their chosen path of healing, be that orthodox or alternative. They've cleared everything from fibroids and tumours to dyslexia and Attention Deficit Disorder; from fertility issues to acne to ulcers; from cancer to arthritis to depression to the common cold! They've cleared cell memories related to childhood illnesses, sports injuries, allergies and asthma – the list goes on and on.

So, while you are partnering your child in undergoing their spiritual journey of liberating their shining potential, very frequently their physical issues will begin to clear naturally. And the great news is that you can use the Kids' Journey alongside whatever health programme your child may be on.

Right now, I offer a five-month Therapists' Accreditation Programme. This is a vigorous, in-depth six-programme course of seminars, each module of which is followed by case studies. Ultimately, each therapist must present 35 case studies before they are eligible for accreditation. The programme has attracted therapists and professionals from a wide range of modalities, including medical doctors, nurses, drug rehabilitation counsellors, alternative and complementary practitioners of all sorts, religious pastors and monks, social workers, school teachers and interested individuals from all walks of life.

What I encourage you to do is use Journeywork alongside your chosen health programme, alongside your career or profession, alongside your chosen faith, alongside your nutritional path. Journeywork is truly integrative and can be used not only with adults but also with children of all ages.

It's very common when doing Journeywork that when you release old limiting patterns and cell memories, the body automatically goes about the natural process of healing – of its own accord. When you address the unresolved emotional issues in life, physical symptoms can lessen or disappear altogether, and overall health, energy and vitality often improve radically. So don't be surprised if your child not only becomes more joyous, free, creative and socially well-adjusted but also free from various physical challenges.

There was one very dramatic case of a five-year-old girl, Raksha, who lived in a village outside Durban in South Africa. Because of the wonderful warm climate there year round, most kids in her neighbourhood spent lots of time outdoors, playing together in the grass with their pets and leading a very natural outdoorsy life. Unfortunately, there was no question of Raksha being able to play outside in the glorious South African sunshine. She was severely allergic to so many things that her mother Janaki couldn't even keep track of them all: cats, dogs, chickens, grass, pollen, dust, mites, chocolate, soya, peanuts, wheat – the list was endless. Janaki lamented that it seemed as if Raksha was allergic to the whole world – to life itself. She had been diagnosed with chronic and acute asthma, and told that she would have to be on medication for the whole of her life. She had to remain indoors most of the time. She was underweight, had a poor appetite, and had become socially fearful and painfully shy.

At school one day, Raksha had an allergic attack so acute that she had an apoplectic fit and was rushed into hospital. Janaki panicked when she received the call from the emergency room. She rushed straight to the hospital to be with her daughter. The doctors were helpful but adamant: they had stabilized Raksha's condition, but there was no choice – she had to be put on strong ongoing medication immediately. When Janaki saw how many drugs they were suggesting, her heart sank. She just couldn't drug up her little girl with so much medication. There had to be another way.

Janaki had read *The Journey* and had successfully cleared her own acute adult acne using the Physical Journey process, so she thought, 'What have I got to lose? Let me give it a try with Raksha.'

In the first Physical Journey process Janaki did with her daughter, Raksha uncovered a memory of when she was only 18 months to two years old. At that time, Janaki had to leave a nanny to take care of her little girl while she was working full-time as a teacher at the local primary school. Apparently the nanny was somewhat inexperienced, but very stern and strict. Every time little Raksha ventured to the screen door, trying the handle to go out into the back garden, the nanny would get fearfully controlling. She was so scared that Raksha would hurt herself and that *she'd* be held to blame that she would admonish the little toddler severely, upbraiding her for even going close to the screen door. But, as you know, little children can often be annoyingly, doggedly persistent and young Raksha made a daily practice of trying to turn the door handle to let herself out. She was fascinated by the grass, the chickens, the dogs and cats. She loved the smell of the mango tree and she just *had* to get out there. The nanny became more and more frustrated and infuriated until, one day, she lashed out verbally. Pointing to the mango tree just outside the door, she said, 'There's a bogey man who lives in that tree! If you ever go out there, he's going to come and get you, and he'll eat you up!' Little Raksha caught her breath. She was terrified, believing every word the nanny said – as small kids usually do.

After this, each day as the little girl went into the kitchen, the nanny would taunt, 'Don't go near that door. He'll eat you for breakfast!' Soon Raksha could only whimper and shake at the thought. She didn't want to go anywhere near that scary door, she wanted to stay safely inside. Eventually, even leaving the house with her parents became terrifying. But, of course, no two-year-old would think of explaining their fears – besides which, doesn't *everyone* know that the bogey man lives out there? So Raksha just internalized her terror, living in a perpetual state of fear any time she got anywhere near the door, or smelled the grass, or heard the hens clucking or the dogs barking – it all reminded her of the bogey man.

Of course Janaki noticed her daughter's unusual aversion to the kitchen door and to leaving the house. She thought it strange, but didn't know what to make of it.

During Raksha's Journey process, not only did she face this old fear but she finally released all the pent-up anger, rage and outrage she felt towards the nanny for controlling her so abusively. In her Change Memory process she received balloons of courage, of the certain knowledge that it is safe and fun outdoors, of the ability to play, laugh and have fun, of self-confidence, the ability to express herself, and so on. And she finally forgave the mean nanny for instilling such debilitating terror in such a sweet and innocent child.

When the process was over, Janaki took her daughter outside and showed her the mango tree, explaining that it had all been a very hurtful lie and that it was, in fact, very beautiful outside. In their spiritual tradition, the mango tree is a sacred tree. No bogey man ever existed.

Later, Janaki spoke to me privately and related how guilty she felt after hearing her child's tearful account of being terrorized by the nanny. She said, 'You know, I had a feeling something was going on, but at the time I just didn't know what to do – I had a full-time job and had to leave her with a nanny. I just feel so upset knowing that she was treated so appallingly.' I suggested that she might like to get an adult Emotional Journey to help her to clear out her own guilt. Thankfully, she did so and she's been at ease with the issue ever since.

Janaki did the Kids' process with Raksha twice more, just for good measure, and only two weeks after being hospitalized, Raksha was *completely allergy free, and has remained so ever since.*

It's now a year later, and Raksha has put on some weight. She's full of energy, life and vigour. She plays happily outdoors with the hens and chicks, dogs and cats, rolling in the grass, playing in the hay, and finally playing happily and healthily with the other kids in the neighbourhood. Janaki says she now eats anything and everything, and has a robustly healthy appetite. Most important, she's no longer fearful and shy. Instead, in Janaki's words, she's 'full of fun, fun, fun!'

Here's a small section of a beautiful letter I received from Janaki:

> *I really do not know whether this letter will do justice to all that I have to say ... for the thanks in my heart and soul and the love brimming over! My daughter Raksha is a healthy normal child who is free from asthma and all the steroids that she would have been on. Her allergies are gone! She is a bouncing bundle of health and vitality.*
>
> *The stress of parents who have an ill child is debilitating as you feel as if the gods have turned their backs on you and you have nowhere to go. This is what both my husband and I felt when Raksha fell ill. Now, almost three years later, she is hale and hearty. The Journey cleared poignant issues and freed her from illness. No medication, no allergies, no hospitals and doctors ... It really feels good.*
>
> *God never forsook us ... He guided us to The Journey ... gently and with love!*

As parents what we most long for is our children's health and well-being.

☼ ☼ ☼

Often, when it comes to physical injuries or accidents, it doesn't occur to us to offer a Journey process to our children. We might wonder, 'How could it possibly be useful? Where's the emotional connection?' If a child falls off her bike, breaks her leg or injures her arm, how could that seemingly random, *external* event be connected to an *internal* emotional issue or block? And yet I've heard countless stories of children whose healing from an accident or injury was greatly hastened by doing Journeywork.

Among them, one particular child stands out. Eight-year-old Robert had fallen and broken his arm. Eventually, he developed an acute infection in the bone and the doctors' prognosis was dire – if this serious infection did not heal within a few weeks, there would be no option but to amputate the entire arm. Ellen, Robert's mother, was overwhelmed by the prospect and desperately began seeking a way to catalyse or speed up the necessary healing. She decided to contact a local therapist and healer whom she knew specialized in Reiki hands-on healing. It could only help.

It so happened that Sandra, the Reiki healer, was partway through our Journey Therapists' Accreditation programme. After she listened to the full account of Robert's condition, she suggested that it might be beneficial for him to have a Kids' Journey process. For Ellen, the thought of her son losing his arm was unthinkable, so she was both grateful and open to trying anything that might help.

Very often people who are skilled in other health or medical modalities incorporate The Journey alongside their chosen field. In this case, Sandra successfully coupled her hands-on healing work with the Kids' Journey.

Below is the full account of what took place in Robert's healing process. The names have been changed to protect everyone's privacy, but this is the first-hand account of the events, written up as a case study by the therapist:

> *Robert is eight years old and lives in Devon with his mother and sister. His mother says that he is often very angry and verbally and physically aggressive to both adults and children alike. In September 2001 he fell and broke his arm, and needed a cast applied. This seemed to have no effect on his destructive moods, which continued as if nothing had happened. In December 2001, a week before his grandfather died, during a very emotional time at home, he knocked his arm at school and started to complain that it was hurting him.*
>
> *It was while he was in Birmingham, waiting for his grandfather's funeral, that he first mentioned that he now had a lump*

in his arm over the place where the break had been. His mother took him to Casualty where, after X-rays, they kept him in hospital and started him on intravenous antibiotics, with the diagnosis that he had acute osteomyelitis, an infection of the bone and bone marrow. He underwent seven days of intensive intravenous antibiotic therapy, then was sent home on oral antibiotics, with the warning that there was a big possibility that he could lose his arm.

At the end of February, his mother asked me if I could give him hands-on healing, as his arm was not improving. I suggested Journey therapy, combined with hands-on healing. Initially, Robert was reluctant to go through it, but we put aside an afternoon when he could come, and I went through the basics of the Kids' Journey process with him, explaining that whatever was said, none of it would be repeated to his mum. If he wanted to share it, that would be up to him. It was only then that he agreed to try.

He went into the Kids' Journey process easily, quickly seeing the space shuttle and raring to get on his way. I asked him who his mentor was, and when he said it was his mum, I asked him if he could think of someone really special, like a hero or an angel. He chose a Pokemon character that I had not heard of. The green button in his shuttle read 'Osteomyelitis' — his word. He was taken to his injured arm, where he described it as feeling 'really crazy in here'. He said that it was very hot and dark, and that he was outside the bone. So he looked for a door and went into the bone.

Once inside, everything was very bright, 'so bright that it can blind you', and very, very hot and sticky. He saw a hole in his arm, and felt the heat coming out of it, making him feel very strange. Looking down at his feet and seeing what shoes he was wearing, he found himself at four years old and in his reception class at school on a hot day. His teacher had not allowed him to have a drink, leaving him feeling sticky, very hot and agitated.

He worked through the Change Memory process without any problem – finding balloons was easy for him. He wanted a balloon to feel strong, one with a voice to be heard, a balloon of fun and one of knowing that everything was OK. Replaying the scene this time, his teacher really heard his requests, let him have plenty to drink and he felt that he was not at all upset this time. During the Campfire Process [which is where kids get the chance to say what they wish they could have said at the time of the memory and empty out any unexpressed emotions, finally coming to forgiveness] *Robert spoke briefly to his teacher, told her that she should listen to him and easily found forgiveness for her.*

After the campfire, when he looked at his arm again, he said that it was no longer hot and that the hole had got smaller. I finished this with a half-hour hands-on healing session on his arm, and he went home. I combined the hands-on healing with The Journey as I believe that healing speeds up the process of whatever is going on with the body. It allows the body to do what it needs to do.

His mother has not brought him back yet, but she is absolutely thrilled, as his entire behaviour has changed radically. He is much calmer.

One month later, Robert went back to see the consultant orthopaedic specialist at Torbay hospital who, after looking at the new set of X-rays, expressed his amazement at the astonishing healing that had taken place. He turned to Robert's mother and said, 'What have you been doing with him? There's virtually no sign that there was ever a break in the arm, let alone an infection.' He added that all that was left was a tiny mark, but that the infection had completely disappeared.

Recently my good friend Zoë told me that her five-year-old son had got really ill just two days before having to perform in a school play. He had a cold and 'flu-like symptoms, and as the play got closer and closer, his symptoms worsened. Zoë began to worry that Lee wouldn't be up to performing and she was sad-dened because he had put so much of himself into it. He was always talking about the play, sharing his apparent excitement, and she knew it was of paramount importance to him and that it would be a big blow if he couldn't be there. Lee's teacher spoke to Zoë privately, after a rehearsal. She said, 'I've noticed that Lee has been terrified of forgetting his lines. I think he's making him-self sick with fear.'

Fortunately for Lee, this wise and experienced teacher continued to encourage him, and her words gave him the courage to go for it, 'flu symptoms and all. It turned out that Lee's performance was fabulous and he was thrilled that he had remembered his lines perfectly. Within an hour of the conclusion of the show, all his symptoms had *completely disappeared*. The teacher explained to Zoë that the best antidote to fear is meeting the fear and working through it, and that she would actively continue to encourage Lee in performing in plays.

Since that time Lee has turned out to be a 'natural'.

I really appreciated hearing Zoë's story, as it points to something we don't often stop to question. How often, when your child has had a cold or the 'flu, have you said to a friend or relative, 'Oh, there's a bug going around the school. I think Sarah caught it off her friend Julie. She's had a cold all week.' We instantly look *out-side* to find where the sickness was 'caught from' and it doesn't occur to us to ask, 'If my eight-year-old daughter is sick, why isn't her six-year-old sister down with it, too? They sleep together in the same room.'

I've begun to think it's possible that sometimes we create an internal environment, a consciousness that is an 'invitation' to get sick. Emotionally, we run ourselves down, and then we are prone to express it through physical symptoms or illness. Journey mums and dads around the world frequently share how cold and 'flu symptoms lessen or disappear almost immediately following a Kids' Journey process.

Some years ago, one child came to the Junior Journey programme so hoarse he could barely speak. He was croaking out his words as if he had laryngitis and his nose was running almost continuously. His mum apologized, saying that Jamie regularly seemed to get throat problems and that she never would have brought him along in this condition if it hadn't been for the fact that she was herself enrolled in the adults' Abundance Retreat that was taking place concurrently with the kids' programme. As it had all happened at the last minute, she just hadn't been able to get a sitter at such short notice and she hoped that Jamie would be OK.

Eight-year-old Jamie was one of the first kids to receive a Kids' Journey. His process was simple and straightforward. In it he went to his throat, which was, 'all scratchy and rough like sandpaper'. The cell memory he uncovered was from when he was five years of age. He was on a family holiday in Spain and had become separated from his mum when they were at a bustling outdoor bazaar. He'd been terrified that he'd lost his mum in a strange place and she might never find him. Eventually a police officer came over and tried to chat with him in broken English until, after what seemed like ages to Jamie, his mum came frantically racing back and they were reunited. Jamie felt bad because he had not stayed by his mum's side and was secretly ashamed that he'd been so terribly frightened by the experience. He thought she might think he was a baby or tell him off, and so all his pent-up fear and anxiety got choked back, caught in his throat. He'd been scared to death, but he had never told anyone.

In his process, not only did Jamie finally experience and release all the stored pent-up fear, he also found a more resourceful way to handle situations like it in the future. In the Change Memory process he received balloons of confidence, courage, self-esteem, trust, the ability to ask for help, the knowledge his mum would return, and the deeper knowledge that his mum loved him more than life itself and she would go to the ends of the Earth to find him, no matter what.

When he replayed the scene with all his new internal resources, he saw clearly how in future he'd handle it much more whole-somely and healthily. He really understood that it helped to share his emotions with his mum and he understood how deeply she loved him. He learned to trust and to ask for help if he needed it.

At the end of his Campfire Process he forgave both his mum and himself for getting lost, and when he went back to look at the rough, sandy surface of his throat, it looked all pink, shiny and healthy. He asked his throat if it had any advice to give him, and it answered that in future he should trust that he is safe and that he should openly express what he is feeling – and that in busy places, it's sensible to keep close to your parents.

Jamie agreed to follow his own deepest wisdom and when the process was over, all hoarseness was gone and he was able to speak clearly. He didn't feel as if there was anything choking or stifling him in his throat any more. By the next day, his runny nose had dried up and his cold had gone completely. Jamie's real-life story is the one I used as the basis for the kids' fairytale process you'll come to later in the book.

In those days, the Junior Journey took place during and alongside the adults' Abundance Retreat, so the children were having their workshop in one part of the building while the grown-ups were down the hall in another room. Usually after lunch on the Sunday we would invite the kids to join the adults, show them their 'before' and 'after' paintings and perform an amusing campfire skit, complete with balloons and painted faces. The kids proudly 'showed off' their paintings, and I felt the adults got the subliminal message: transformation can be fun, easy and joyous – you don't need to make hard work of it!

On this occasion Jamie's mum was stunned to see her son's 'chronic throat problem' disappear and she was so proud of the part he played in the skit.

Six-year-old Oliver held up his 'before' and 'after' paintings, and the 'after' looked just like a shell. A medical doctor attending the Abundance Retreat gasped when he saw it. He asked if he could speak to the child and went up to Oliver, saying, 'That's an anatomically correct picture of the cochlea in the ear – you can't have taken anatomy lessons at your age, can you?'

'*What* kind of lessons?' Oliver replied. 'I just went in here [pointing to his ear], and I found this shell inside. It looked all gunky at first, but now it looks all clean and shiny.' He showed the doctor the rays of light he'd painted coming from the shell in the 'after' picture, as if that explained everything!

Everyone smiled at his innocence. We were all awed at how powerful the body wisdom is and couldn't help but notice how natural it all seemed.

Sometimes your little ones will draw anatomically accurate pictures of what they see inside. At other times, the soul speaks more poetically, or in metaphor, and the pictures will be more of a representation of what it *felt* like inside. In either case, it is extraordinary to hear our children describe in graphic living-colour detail the part of the body they have visited.

Healing can be a magical and wondrous experience, especially if you are open and innocent. Your own body wisdom is eager to work with you in clearing these old issues and it goes about the process of healing quite naturally.

When it comes to teenagers' healing with The Journey, I almost always recommend they read the original *Journey* book and if they feel drawn to the work, attend the full Journey Intensive weekend.

I was recently in Auckland, offering the first Journey Intensive weekend in New Zealand. A lovely 17 year old and her mother came to share their extraordinary story of healing with some of the trainers. A year before, Yoki had been having terrible headaches and when a brain scan was done, it was discovered that she had a brain tumour. Yoki's mum was beside herself, frantic to help her daughter any way she could and, as so often happens, at exactly that time *The Journey* landed in her lap. She read it from cover to cover and asked her daughter to give it a read. When Yoki was through with the book, she put it down and said rather matter-of-factly to her mum that she was going to heal from the tumour. Thrilled to be able to do something to assist, her mother turned to the back of the book and found the process sheets. Over the next few weeks mother and daughter did several processes.

When they arrived at the weekend course, they were both feeling so proud –Yoki had gone for a brain scan three days earlier and no trace of the tumour remained. To Yoki, it seemed totally natural that this would be the result. She had been absolutely and resolutely *certain* she would heal.

At the Journey Intensive both Yoki and her mother received more in-depth instruction on how to use Journeywork in *all* aspects of their lives. As I watched them both, I realized that the mother was now the one who really needed the work; she'd gone through so much worry about her daughter and it was a great relief for her to finally offload her own burdens and emotional baggage. By the end of the weekend, both Yoki and her mum were glowing.

Sometimes, when our loved ones are going about the process of healing, the first thing we can do in partnering them is to clean out our own emotional baggage, fears and the burden of feeling responsible, so that we can be of more joyous, open and wholesome support.

If your child or loved one is undergoing a healing process, I strongly encourage you to join them. It's more empowering to be part of the emotional clearing process than to be just a concerned bystander. We *all* have our issues to clear and in The Journey we open deeply into the vast presence of peace inside. From that boundless love, we are better able to support others in becoming free, because we too are free.

You have nothing to lose except some of your own emotional baggage and, who knows, in the process some of your own physical issues may begin to heal.

> Hi my name is Ella and I'm 10 years old. I had a problem that when my mum got the flu I started to feel scared of something that I didn't know and insecure. The Journey helped me by giving me the courage to not be scared or insecure and to know that my mum will get better. After I felt very light like a ball and happy that I scared away my problem.   Ella

5

Issues of Death and Loss

Often when we think of children, it doesn't occur to us that they might have to face such a tragic event as a death early on in life, but nearly all of us will have some brush with death before we reach our teens – either a distant relative passes away, a friend's family member dies or perhaps someone close to us perishes. Car accidents happen, cancer strikes, sports accidents occur and even suicides take place within families. Yet, somehow we view this as an issue to 'hide from the children' – 'Don't tell them, they need to be protected from this. They aren't emotionally equipped to understand. It's too upsetting.' It's almost as if death is taboo, something that is only spoken about in hushed voices and behind closed doors. This gives children the clear impression that something is wrong with death, that you shouldn't have to feel the natural feelings of loss or grief, that it shouldn't be spoken about.

Usually, if this kind of attitude is prevalent around kids, I look to the parents to see what is really taking place. Often it's the parent, not the child, who hasn't come to terms with the concept of death – they have unresolved issues within themselves and they are trying to protect their children from having to face what they themselves cannot bear the thought of facing. So they try to sweep it all under the carpet, usually unsuccessfully.

Death is a natural part of life that children witness and experience quite regularly: the fly or the beetle is squirming on its back, clearly in its death throes, and suddenly the body goes inert and Mummy says, 'It's dead. We need to sweep it up and put it into the dustbin.' Plants wither and die, and often pets will pass on due to old age or accidents. Goldfish are regularly found floating at the top of the fish tank and get flushed down the loo, and hamsters and rabbits are particularly short-lived, often ending up buried in our gardens.

Even if we try to shield our kids from the worst of the news, death is in cartoons, fairytales, videos and computer games; it's in newspapers, magazines and everyday conversational phone calls. Death is everywhere, and yet parents so often want to 'protect' children from this inevitable and very natural part of life. In so doing we disable our children. I can't tell you how many Journey processes I've done with adults whose campfire processes were all about letting go of the absolute fury they felt at having the death of a loved one swept under the carpet or made light of. They often say that it was as if they weren't allowed to feel all that they felt at the time because it was all hushed up and never spoken of again. This can be the worst form of suppression.

I often hear words such as 'I was never given a chance to grieve', 'No one ever explained to me what happened', 'I found out much later from someone else', 'I feel so robbed', 'I never got a chance to say goodbye, to complete with her.' What is inevitably revealed at campfires is that it was the *parents* who couldn't cope with the loss and therefore were projecting their fears onto the kids in the guise of protecting them from having to face the upsetting news.

Trying to protect our children from life's natural cycles only makes it more difficult for them when they actually have to face the real-life loss of a loved one.

I vividly remember one very moving case of this. I was having a joyous, lively discussion with a beautiful five-year-old American girl, Casey, and she was asking what it looked like where I lived. I told her that where I was staying in England was very beautiful and was close to a town called Windsor, where a real live queen lived in a magnificent ancient castle. I described the castle in great detail and said that the queen's grandchildren went to school at nearby Eton and that it was one of her favourite castles because she could see her grandchildren there. I explained how they would fly a special flag whenever the queen came to stay in the castle and I told Casey that if ever she came to visit, I would take her to see the castle. On hearing this, she innocently asked, 'Does the princess live there too?'

'No,' I answered simply and honestly. 'The princess died in a car accident two years ago.'

Casey's mother, who is normally easy-going and deeply spiritual, visibly blanched and urgently signalled me to stop speaking about the castle. Bewildered, I followed her lead, as she adamantly gestured for me to step aside and speak with her privately. In a fierce whisper she said, 'We don't talk about such things. Casey is way too young to have to deal with the concept of death. She's only five. We try to protect her from such upsetting subjects.'

'But death is a natural part of life. It happens all around us, all the time.'

'She's too young to hear about such things. When Princess Diana died, we didn't even turn on the television or bring home magazines or newspapers. We didn't want to expose Casey to such upsetting news.'

'But wasn't it talked about at school? It was all over the news – surely the other kids must have said something.'

'No – most of the other mothers in her school agreed not to discuss it in front of the kids. In my house I don't let the children
watch *any* violent television shows, not even cartoons. I won't
even read fairytales that have bad endings – if the princess dies, I
just tell Casey that she's gone to sleep. I always change them. I feel
very adamant; I just don't think children should be exposed to
death at this age. Life is hard enough. They are so innocent; they
should be allowed to stay that way a while longer.'

Knowing that one of their cats had passed away a couple of years
earlier, I quietly wondered how Casey's mother had explained that
to her.

In some respects, though, I could readily sympathize with Casey's
mum. I too feel adamant that children should not have to be
exposed to the harsh violence that is shown in most of our action
films, and even on the news. It's too traumatizing at such an early
age. Even fairytales can be scary for little children and I fervently
wish there were more uplifting and healing ones (like the one in
this book!) for children to listen to.

And yet it really appeared in this instance that there was something deeper going on for the mother. Car accidents happen every
day; surely, for this very reason, children are warned not to step
onto the road where there is traffic and to cross over only where

it is safe to do so. It appeared to me that Casey's mum was more uncomfortable with the subject of death than her daughter.

A year later, when Casey was only six years old, a tragedy did indeed beset their life. One of Casey's closest schoolfriends, Natalie, broke her arm. While in hospital, she contracted a rare and virulent infection that got into her bones and she died suddenly at the tender age of six.

The whole school was absolutely devastated. The teachers made every attempt to help the children come to terms with their tragic loss and parents were invited to participate in that healing process. Of course, all the parents had to deal with their own fears of 'What if this had been my child?' Natalie had been a perfectly healthy child. The thought was unbearable. So the kids not only had to deal with their own grief, loss and confusion but they could also feel their parents' fears rippling through as well.

When I spoke to Casey on the phone, her voice sounded plaintive. 'I didn't know little kids could die,' she said, 'I thought it just happened to old people.' Casey was clearly not only pained at the loss, but also because she felt that life had 'duped' her. No one had let her know that accidents happen, and when this one took place she felt betrayed by life itself.

When I spoke to her mother, who was clearly nursing her own fears as well as trying to cope with Casey's, she told me how deeply it had hit the whole family. 'Casey and Natalie were really close. Casey's been withdrawn and depressed ever since it happened, and she's not sleeping well.'

Of course I reassured Casey's mum that it is natural that Casey would feel the loss of her friend so deeply. Both children and adults feel such loss and fear acutely; we all need time for grieving. What was so upsetting in this instance was that Casey was not *openly* experiencing her grief, she was hiding herself away and *shutting herself down.*

When I heard that part, I explained to her mum that the shutdown is not natural; that if kids are open, they usually feel things rawly and express their feelings naturally. I wondered if perhaps something else might be going on and I suggested that it might be a good idea to do a short and sweet Kids' Journey with Casey. I said, 'You don't have to do the whole Kids' Journey. Just ask Casey to close her eyes and let the whole room be filled with light, then let her imagine a warm and cosy campfire and invite her young friend Natalie along. See if there is anything Casey needs to say to complete with her dear friend.'

Her mother, who is a beautiful and conscious soul, did just that. That night, she sat down with Casey and said, 'Why don't we say some prayers for Natalie? Let's imagine the whole room filled with love and light, and we'll welcome her to join us at a beautiful bonfire.'

Casey, who is naturally a very spiritual child, was relieved to be given a process that she could actually participate in. So they all sat by the imaginary campfire and then the truth came out: Casey really loved her friend, but apparently about one week before Natalie broke her arm, some other kids at school had been making fun of her and Casey had stood silently by and done nothing to stop the cruel teasing. When it was over she felt ashamed, but didn't get the chance to say how sorry she was. She hadn't helped her good friend when it mattered, and shortly after that the friend had died. Now she just wished she could turn back the clock.

Casey, in her childlike way, explained all this to Natalie, who was sitting by her imaginary campfire. Natalie looked luminous, surrounded by light, filled with love. She indicated to Casey that it really didn't matter; she didn't take it personally and anyway she felt very at peace and was basking in the love-light. Casey's face visibly relaxed as she received Natalie's wordless forgiveness and at about this time she fell into the first deep sleep she'd had since her friend had died.

Later that week, Casey's mother told me that by the day after the process Casey's depression had lifted and now she seemed in a much healthier and easy place in herself.

I was so thrilled Casey had been respected in her grief and invited healthily to face and clear her unaddressed issue – that she'd finally completed with her friend and shared what she hadn't been able to say to Natalie before she had died. She finally found peace, and has come to know for certain that wherever Natalie is, she is surrounded by light and love and is free.

☼ ☼ ☼

Children need the same chance to complete as adults do. If we can put aside our own fears (or better still, face and clear them in a Journey process), then we can better support our children in finding peace, even in the face of such tragic loss.

A similar situation happened with a woman in New York City, shortly after September 11th when the World Trade Center towers went down. It happened that I was launching *The Journey* in America at the time. On September 10th 2001, 600 press releases with 600 books were sent out by my publishers to the national media and press. On September 11th my book was buried news, eclipsed (as well it should have been) by the catastrophic loss of nearly 3,000 lives. Yet I was aware that I was in America at just that moment for a reason. As soon as I saw the news, I knew that I *had* to somehow help the families of those who had died. So I cancelled all my paying seminars and one month after the attack my team and I went to New York City to offer a free-of-charge Journey event to those who had been affected by the devastation.

I felt called to help in any way I could because of what the field of psycho-neuro-immunology has discovered about trauma and our immune systems. As you know, if we experience a catastrophic event and we shut down our natural emotional response, our bodies release chemicals that will block certain cell receptors, rendering them unable to communicate properly with other cells, and our whole body chemistry begins to shift out of its natural healthy balance.

One result of this, simply put, is that as we shut ourselves down emotionally, we begin to shut down our whole immune system. Three weeks after 9/11 I read in a New York newspaper that hospitals were full and that doctors and health therapists overstretched – *not* because of the emergencies due to the actual disaster, but because people with *existing* conditions had found that their symptoms had suddenly got worse. Those who already had cancer found it became aggressive; those who had asthma found it became acute; those who had chronic fatigue became incapacitated; those who had arthritis became immobilized; those with depression became overwhelmed. Pre-existing conditions, both physical and emotional, worsened dramatically, and doctors' surgeries, hospitals and therapists' practices quickly became stretched to the max.

In the face of so much trauma, few of us knew how to deal wholesomely with the intense grief and fear that arose, so most of us relied on our old tried and trusted strategy – stuff it back down, hope it goes away and get back to work. But this time the trauma was so great and the repercussions so acute that our cell receptors started getting blocked, our bodies' chemistry changed and we overwhelmed our health services with calls for help.

I realized that New York needed help of a different kind – help to clear out those cell memories, release the trauma and forgive so that we could grieve naturally and let our bodies heal in the process.

In the middle of October, 20 of my staff and trainers flew into NYC from Australia, South Africa and the United Kingdom to support the free-of-charge Journey workshop, and it was a deeply moving, very raw and profoundly healing event. Firemen's wives came, families and friends of the deceased came, nurses, teachers and ministers came. More than one third of the room had lost a loved one. And everyone knew someone who had died. As the grief was still so very raw, it was a very tender and sensitive workshop.

Nearly all the 200 people who attended found the courage to undergo the Physical Journey and by the end of the day everyone looked quietly relieved and much more at peace.

One woman shared an unusual experience. The cell memory she uncovered went back to when she was eight years old. At that time her sister had died. Like so many parents, hers didn't know how to help her through the grief process. She was left out of all the family's discussions of death and was not given a chance to feel and express her own grief. Most of her parents' grieving took place privately, behind closed doors. The little girl felt completely excluded from the obvious grieving that was taking place and didn't feel she knew how to say goodbye to her sister – she had no idea how to complete. To top it all off, on the day of the funeral, her parents felt she would be better off missing it, that it would be 'too traumatizing' for an eight year old, and so she was left completely alone in her apartment, excluded from the family's ceremonies for her sister.

In her memory she vividly remembered looking out of the window and seeing her sister's coffin in a hearse, as the funeral procession solemnly and silently passed by. She remembered feeling absolutely desolate, utterly alone. Sitting in the midst of her grief, this little eight-year-old girl felt that when it came to tragedy, everyone had deserted her – no one was there to hold her hand and comfort her, or even to fully explain what was happening. In her mind's eye, this cell memory appeared on one side of a split screen.

On the other side of the split screen appeared the current memory of the Twin Towers coming down. Once again, she was all alone. She had been getting ready to go to work when she had turned on the television and her whole world had stopped. Lost and alone, frozen in front of the television screen, once again she was witnessing tragedy without a hand to hold or anyone to turn to. She was running that same old childhood pattern – this time in the face of a current catastrophe.

She said that all her life she'd felt so desperately alone. She'd learned at eight years old that if tragedy ever came no one would be there for her. And of course, for her, history repeated itself.

During her Journey process, not only did she finally face and release all the past pain, but once and for all she forgave her parents for not including her in the grieving and completion process. She felt at peace with her parents, and from that peace she came to a profound realization. 'What was I thinking?' she later shared out loud. 'I'm not alone – I'm in a city *full* of millions of people like me, all longing to reach out and help each other. I have so many friends I could have called instead of sitting frozen in front of the television. Every one of them would have been there for me, but because I had this whole "loner victim identity" it never occurred to me that I didn't have to wait until people reached out to me – *I could have reached out to them!* I've *never* been alone! And I'll never buy into that "lonesome stranger" story again – it's just *not* the truth!'

The whole audience applauded and I think everyone in that moment thought of all the times in recent weeks when they'd felt alone and how isolated in our own grief we all felt – when in fact there was a whole world out there with arms outstretched.

All of us, adults and children alike, deserve the chance to go through the grieving and completion process – wholesomely, as an embrace, instead of in exclusion.

Recently there was a Junior Journey in Melbourne, Australia. Kim Davis, a schoolteacher who is extremely creative in her use of Journeywork with kids and has developed all kinds of ingenious teachers' aids, headed it up with other Accredited Therapists and trainers.

One boy arrived with a tragic story of having lost *both* his parents. His guardians loved him dearly, but didn't know how to help him get through his pain. He had completely shut down towards them and was hardly willing to communicate. After his Journey process, his guardians wrote to one of the trainers to say that he is now so much freer and warmer – that when they drop him off at school, he now thanks them and wishes them a lovely day, openly reaching out to them, whereas in the past he would close the car door in silence and walk sulking into school. They were thrilled that a single day could bring about such a significant transformation after such a traumatic event.

There is a particularly moving story about one child who experienced the double deaths of loved ones *on the same day*. A year before coming to the Junior Journey, Joe lost both his dad and his dog Rusty on the same day. From that day forward Joe fell silent. He was incapable of speaking. Of course his family were deeply concerned for him; they tried everything – he went to therapy, had medical hypnosis, he underwent neuro-linguistic programming therapy, but nothing seemed to work. He just couldn't utter a syllable – he was literally speechless.

When Joe arrived at the Junior Journey programme, I said to the head trainer that he was not stupid, he just couldn't speak. I recommended that she get very creative in working with him. As most of his process would be taking place internally, with closed eyes, she needed to agree in advance hand gestures to signal what was going on and she needed to leave enough space at the campfire for a non-verbal internal conversation to take place. I suggested that it might be a good idea to explain to Joe in advance the entire Kids' Journey and how it works, so that he could relax with it and carry out the process in his mind's eye in his own way. And I reminded her that, as Rusty could only bark a response, she needed to give the dog a balloon of communication, so that Joe could clearly understand his replies at the campfire.

Joe listened carefully to the instructions and agreed on certain hand gestures. Finally the therapist asked him to close his eyes. She read the Kids' Journey like a guided meditation or fairytale and kept checking throughout the process that Joe was with her – 'Can you see the steps? … Good … Are you inside the shuttle yet? … Great' – as Joe gestured his responses. She asked him to indicate where in his body the space shuttle had landed and he pointed to his throat. During the Change Memory process she had to keep asking, 'Would this balloon help? Would that balloon help?' and Joe agreed to most but not all of them – he knew intuitively *exactly* what would have helped him in the scene. When it came to the campfire conversation, the therapist wondered how it would go – obviously she didn't know the content, as it was all done silently in Joe's private, internal experience. Gently, she kept asking questions. 'Is your dad there? ... Good ... Then let him speak now ... Is Rusty there? ... Good ... Does he have his balloon of communication? ... Great ... Then let him speak.' Joe gestured in response to each question and the therapist left plenty of time between each question for each person to express their emotions. Joe had not cried since the deaths, but tears welled up in his eyes and a single tear rolled down one cheek.

To the therapist it *seemed* to go beautifully, but she couldn't really tell until afterwards, when Joe opened his eyes and *spoke his first words*. He told her exactly what had taken place during his journey. His shuttle had arrived in his throat and there was an area that looked dark, tight and constricted. When he went over to that area, immediately the cell memory that was stored there came flooding and he went back to the day his dad and his dog died. His father had died suddenly, unexpectedly and Joe had never had the chance to speak to him. He had only one question to ask of his father: 'Why did you leave without saying goodbye?' His dad responded, 'Well, son, I didn't really have a choice, but, you know, I never really left. If you look inside your heart, you'll find I've stored all my love for you there. I'm always with you – right inside you.'

When it came to Rusty, Joe asked the same exact question: 'Why did *you* leave without saying goodbye?' With his balloon of communication, Rusty was able to answer easily, 'Well, I didn't have a choice either – it was an accident – but, you know, I never left you either. If you look up at the night sky, you'll find my shape there outlined in the stars. I watch over you every night while you're sleeping.'

Fully realizing that both his father's love and his dog's love were always with him, Joe was finally able to come to peace. Before the campfire disappeared, his father said to him, 'Any time you want to speak to me, just go inside your heart, find me there and I'll meet you at the campfire.'

Only 20 minutes had gone by, but Joe had heard what he needed to hear to finally come to terms with their deaths. He's been speaking freely and easily ever since – and now I'm the proud owner of a T-shirt he painted for me with a dog outlined in stars.

Very often young children need to understand, to have simple answers to simple questions. Sometimes those answers can only come from within, from their own wisdom. I wish we could all learn how to process the loss of a loved one as simply as Joe did. His innocence and openness are his greatest allies, and can teach us all.

6

Using The Journey in Everyday Life

As parents, we can often be happily engaged in an ordinary family outing when some unexpected trauma happens right before our eyes. It might not be our immediate response to think of Journeywork *at that moment* and yet using the principles of the work spontaneously, in the very midst of crisis, can be extraordinarily effective. It always brings a sense of wholeness, release and completion to the issue and helps put it into perspective. More importantly, you are freeing and clearing the issue *before* it gets stored in the body and ends up as a limiting, conditioned response sometime in the future.

Once you are genuinely familiar with the various aspects of the process, the tools will come in very handy – sometimes at the most unexpected moments.

A couple of years ago, I had quite a dramatic experience of this first hand. I went out for a Sunday afternoon's boating on a beautiful lake on Sydney's North Shore with my dear friend Samantha and her wonderfully bright and vivacious six-year-old daughter Jade. We moored our little dinghy next to a lovely outdoor restaurant with lush green lawns and a glorious lakeside garden full of outdoor sculptures, topiary and a rose arbour.

Luckily for us, we got one of the last tables available and once we'd placed our orders for lunch, Jade asked if she could play in the garden while we waited for our meals to arrive. Jade is not just a bright child, she is one of those precocious kids – you know the type, six going on sixteen, very wise, wonderfully practical and direct, and extremely responsible for her age, or any age for that matter. Our table was positioned so that we could peer over the patio into the garden and watch her as she played, so Samantha warmly agreed to Jade's request. She cautioned her daughter that she was not to go anywhere near the steps that led to the lake and Jade agreed very amenably. We both knew from her congruent response that she would fully obey her mother's reasonable instructions.

Jade went into the garden and began running and skipping about and we were delighted to watch her natural ease in nature. While keeping a watchful eye on her, we were laughing together about something when suddenly we heard a piercing scream and in an instant realized it was Jade. We'd only just taken our eyes off her. We rushed out into the garden to find her lying on the ground, grasping her leg, whimpering and covered in potting soil, with the remains of a *huge* cement flower basin scattered around her. The urn must have weighed *at least* 100 pounds before it had smashed.

Quickly I reached down to check Jade's legs for any broken bones or gashes and noticed that a big bruise was already beginning to bloom. As I moved each toe and checked for movement in Jade's ankles, Samantha tried to explain to the now frantic restaurant staff that everything was fine, it was just a mishap – no broken bones or serious injury. She offered to pay for the damage, the staff kindly declined and everyone sighed a big sigh of relief that Jade was alright – she was a bit battered and shaken, but definitely OK.

Eventually the staff drifted back to their tasks in the restaurant and I tenderly helped Jade to her feet. She was putting on a very brave face and yet I could see that she'd been in fear for her life. Physically she seemed fine, but emotionally she was clearly in some unvoiced turmoil.

As we sat at lunch, we spoke openly together about what had happened and I tried to draw Jade out, coaxing her into expressing what she was *really feeling*. But instead she described in detail *what had taken place* – she had wanted to climb on top of the pedestal to get a better look at the flowers in the big stone basin and she hadn't realized that the top wasn't attached to the pedestal. So when she grabbed the rim of the basin, it all came toppling down.

Upon hearing that, I blanched, realizing it could have landed directly on her, breaking a leg or even killing her. I knew intuitively that Jade realized this too. She had probably been afraid she was going to die.

Though Jade was accurate in relating *what had happened*, I could see she seemed unable to share the truth of her *emotional feelings*, which kept darting across her sweet face as she gingerly and quietly went about eating lunch. I could see she was suffering and yet she just didn't know how to express what she was feeling.

Finally, not knowing what else to do, I said, 'Jade, I've had it with that basin. I'm going over there to give it a good talking to. Here, take my hand and let's go tell this urn exactly what we think of it for scaring you in this way!' She jumped down off her chair, grabbed my hand and together we marched back out to the garden to give that urn a piece of our minds.

Loudly, I began scolding the basin, chiding it for scaring Jade, telling it that it was bad for falling down and that it should *never, never* try to scare someone like that again. I pretended that, we were together at a campfire, just like in the Journey process, but this one was happening in real life. Jade began to chime in, as I encouraged her to let all of her feelings out. She shouted alongside me until we were both empty of all emotion and then, spontaneously, she burst into laughter. Together we laughed and laughed and laughed.

Then Jade said to me, 'I feel sorry for that basin. It must feel terrible. It didn't want to hurt me or scare me. It's not the basin's fault. We should forgive it – it must feel really bad.'

So together we forgave the basin. We said we knew that it didn't mean to hurt Jade and we were sorry it had got broken. Then I asked, 'I wonder how we could best help this urn – to make it safer in the future?'

Jade said, 'We should tell the restaurant staff that they should put up a little sign that reads "Children, please don't climb on me – I'm not stable" and then draw a picture of a child climbing with a red line through it, for the kids too young to read. That way both kids and the basin would feel safe.'

Once Jade had passed on her message and learning to the restaurant staff, she felt emotionally complete. She'd emptied out the fear for her life and the upset and trauma it had brought up for her.

She'd reached a place of forgiveness and compassion with the urn, and a place of self-forgiveness as well. Finally, she'd come to recognize the lesson the urn was trying to teach her and she was able to use that lesson to help other kids who might end up in her shoes.

On the ride home Jade seemed joyously at peace, completely free and whole. In the car, I asked her if she would be willing to do a little closed-eye process with me. She had already successfully completed her 'campfire' with the urn, yet I felt she could still benefit from a Change Memory process to positively programme in healthy responses for the future. I wanted to make sure that she didn't become 'phobic' about climbing, that she'd learn instead that, even though it was *in*appropriate to climb on that specific urn, tree-house climbing and climbing on monkey bars were perfectly safe and fun. So I asked Jade to close her eyes, go to a campfire and ask a mentor what kinds of balloons might be useful in future. She named perfectly appropriate ones: play, fun, trust, safety, looking for secure steps to step on, checking to see that everything was safe, self-esteem and courage. She breathed all the qualities in. Then I asked her to imagine climbing up on something with all her balloons, to put that scene up on the movie screen and play it the way it *would happen in the future,* with all these beautiful and helpful internal qualities.

Jade described her scene very colourfully. She was climbing up her favourite tree, a tree that she is allowed to climb on and that she already knows is safe. She was checking each step of the way to make sure that the branches were still safe to climb on. When she got up to the tree house she felt that it was so much fun to be up there, all cosy in her own special place. She knew inside that she'd been thoughtful and sensible about her climb, and that made playing in the tree house much more fun. She even said she'd like to help other kids learn to climb safely and thoughtfully, and that being safe makes you feel good about what you are doing.

Once the Change Memory process was complete and she'd forgiven herself for her past mistake, her campfire concluded naturally. She opened her eyes and she was absolutely beaming, full of self-confidence and joy.

Samantha told me a week later that since her process Jade had spent the whole week in pure bliss. She'd never seen her daughter so free and confident.

When I got off the phone, I thought about what *could* have happened: that trauma could have stunted Jade's natural athleticism and love of climbing. It could have made her fearful of taking healthy risks and attempting physical challenges or, worse still, Jade could have generalized her fear – she could have become fearful of rose gardens, statues, lakes, boats, even restaurants. Very often, children will have a fright, forget where they got the fear from and then generalize it to any situation that remotely resembles or is associated with the initial traumatic event. Instead, Jade is soaring in healthy confidence in herself and I've subsequently been delighted to hear that she's taken up gymnastics!

On hearing Jade's story, my close friend Cliff remarked how it reminded him of what he'd done as a child. While on holiday at the age of six, he'd had an extremely scary experience of nearly drowning in the sea. From that point onward, whenever his parents said, 'We're going on holiday,' he'd immediately ask, 'Where?' And when they'd reply that they were going to the seaside, or a lake, or a pool, or anywhere near water, he'd casually reply, 'Oh, I don't really want to go there. I'm not that fussed about holidays.' As well as haivng developed a fear of water and swimming, he'd generalized his one-off experience to mean *all* holidays were scary. He'd forgotten where it came from, he just knew that he didn't really like holidays.

It was not until Cliff was in his early fifties and did Journeywork that he finally freed himself from that fear. Now, in his mid-fifties, he regularly joins us on our holidays in Byron Bay, Australia, just loves swimming in the ocean, has just become a certified scuba diver, and is even learning to surf!

But why wait that long?

About two years ago we had an experience with Kevin's son Mark that was very similar to Cliff's. We had spent a sunny week in Lech, Austria, on a skiing holiday, when on the morning we were leaving to return home a snow squall came out of nowhere. Within minutes the streets were piled high with ten or twelve inches of snow and snowploughs were out everywhere trying to cope with the huge 'dump'.

We needed to drive to Munich to catch a flight to England, so we started out early, leaving plenty of time to crawl along at a snail's pace, following ploughs if needed and taking the one road available out of the Alps. The traffic was creeping along – cars were leaving *en masse* before we all got snowed in. The roads were treacherous and we all sensibly travelled in first gear at under ten miles per hour. We were crawling down the mountain, barely moving, when our car began to slide. Gently, Kevin pumped the brakes, but there was no possibility of stopping – unbeknownst to us, the car rental company had fitted summer tyres to our car, not the winter tyres normally used for Alpine driving. We had no grip whatsoever, even though all the cars around us were doing fine, and our car slid into the rear of the car in front. We all stepped out and checked the car we had collided with. It was completely dent-free, the only damage being a bent number-plate. But ours looked liked a crushed accordion – drivable, but distinctly squashed in the front.

Mark sat silently in the back seat while we spoke to the driver of the other car and exchanged details. Once we were back on the road, I turned to look at him and he was white. I urged him to share what he was really feeling, but of course the standard 'Nothing. I'm OK' response came out. Yet his complexion belied his words.

'You sure, Mark? You look a little pale.'

'Nah, I'm OK.'

I began to share with Mark how *I* really felt – that the experience had given me quite a scare, that my heart was pounding and my breath was a little shallow and that my body was only just beginning to adjust to the fact that we were all, in fact, perfectly safe.

'Is your heart pounding?' I asked.

'Yeah, I think I got a bit scared.'

'That's natural,' I replied. 'What really came up for you, Mark?'

'Well, I noticed the cliff to the left-hand side and I thought we might go over it. I thought we could die.'

'How did that honestly make you feel?'

'Really scared, I think.'

'That's natural, Mark. The same thought occurred to me. Let your body know it's safe – nothing dangerous actually happened. It's natural for the fear to come up and wash through us.'

Mark seemed much more at ease as I encouraged him to give me a blow-by-blow account of his true feelings and when I asked, 'What is the real truth about what is here now?' he said, 'Well, the truth is we are safe. We were only going about five miles per hour and it's really only the car that got hurt.'

The colour came back to his cheeks and for the rest of the ride he seemed more open. Yet he still seemed quieter than usual. Eventually, after our short flight back to the UK, Kev dropped me off and drove Mark back home to his mum. On the M4 motorway, they began to chat privately about the holiday they'd just been on. Mark, who for the whole week away had been through the roof with excitement, seemed indifferent about the trip and softly indicated that he didn't really like skiing that much. It was abundantly clear to Kevin that Mark had subconsciously generalized his fear of death in the car accident and had applied it to the entire ski holiday!

Kev asked Mark if he'd be willing to play with a Change Memory process right there in the car. Mark shrugged OK, and so they started.

The resource balloons Mark chose were: knowledge that he was safe, trust, knowledge that he survived, a sense of humour and fun, courage and self-confidence.

When Mark played the accident scene again, only this time with his helpful internal qualities, he felt safe, courageous and actually had a sense of humour about it all. He noticed how funny the guy in front had looked and how friendly he had been, how the car seemed to be doing its own slow-motion skating dance and that in fact no one had been hurt: we were all safe. After he opened his eyes, he finally looked his natural shiny self. Not surprisingly, he admitted that he actually loved skiing.

This year he can barely wait to go back. It's his top favourite thing on Earth to do and he talks about it with great excitement whenever we mention our next trip to Lech.

Once you've got the 'knack' of it you'll find that freely using individual parts of The Journey or using the entire Kids' Journey process can be useful in just about any traumatic situation. As a matter of fact, you might even want to use it on yourself!

A few years ago, Kevin had quite a different situation arise with Mark and he was able to successfully use Journey tools in his everyday conversation. I asked Kev to write the story directly from his own experience. Here's the first-hand account:

> *We were driving home, chatting enthusiastically about the vintage cars we'd seen in the automobile museum, when there was a natural lull in our conversation. My mind wandered and I casually remarked to Mark, my then eight-year-old son, 'You know, I've been having a bit of trouble with my nose. I have something called a "deviated septum" and it makes it difficult to breathe.' I demonstrated the difficulty I was having. 'When I'm in California this summer, I think I'm going to get an operation to get it fixed.'*
>
> *Mark didn't respond. He remained silent for a few minutes and seemed to be lost in his own thoughts.*
>
> *Eventually, glancing across at him, I noticed that his body*

language had shifted. He had slumped down in his seat and was gazing out of the side window.

'What's up?' I asked. 'Anything the matter?'

'Nothing,' was his reply. He turned further away from me and gazed more intently at the scenery.

'No, really,' I quizzed, 'what's the matter? I can see something's going on.'

'Nothing.' This time in a 'leave me alone' tone.

I pulled the car over to the side of the road and switched the engine off. Turning towards him, I said softly, 'OK, so what's the problem? I can see something is bothering you, but I don't know what it is.'

Again, 'Nothing,' but now in a tone simultaneously defiant and plaintive.

'Whoa,' I replied very gently and slowly, sliding down in my own seat so I could be at his height. 'That doesn't sound like an honest answer to me. I can tell a lot of things by the way you are using your body, for instance by the way your shoulders are

*slumped, the way your head is dropped and the way you are turning away from me and looking down — all these things tell me that something is wrong. And you know, as your dad, part of my job is to care for you and to help you in life — and I can't help you unless you're willing to let me know what's going on inside your world. So, if there **was** something wrong, what might that be? If you **were** feeling something inside, what feeling might that be? What's the truth of how you're feeling?'*

*Mark erupted into uncontrolled sobbing. His whole body heaved, racked with emotion. I had never seen him cry so fiercely, so unabashedly. I waited silently for a few minutes, until the sobbing eased, then quietly asked, 'So what's here? What's this **really** about?'*

'I'm afraid,' he reluctantly whispered, 'that if you go into hospital for an operation you'll die. Then I won't have a daddy.'

My own tears welled up.

I knew that his grandfather had a severe fear of hospitals, but had no idea that Mark had picked up on it so strongly and internalized it so vividly. He went on to explain that he believed that when anyone went into hospital, the chances were they wouldn't come out alive.

'Oh, I see,' I eventually managed. 'So you're afraid that if I go into hospital for an operation I might die.'

'Yes.'

'Well,' I continued, 'let's see how we can work this out.' I explained that what I needed was only a tiny operation and that it was very, very safe. I would only need to be in hospital for a day, probably not even overnight. And I reassured Mark that I would **never** do anything that was dangerous to my health or a risk to my life.

'What if I promised to do lots of research so I can find out the easiest and safest way to get my nose fixed so I can breathe prop-erly? Would that help?'

'A bit,' he answered.

'And what if I promised to discuss everything with you before going ahead? And what if I promised that you and I will **have** to be in complete agreement that it's safe and OK, before I get **anything** done: that we'd **both** need to agree? Would that help?'

'Yes.' This time I could see that his body had relaxed, and he turned to face me. 'It would be OK if we both agree.'

'Right,' I said, 'it's a deal. I'll find out everything I can, and I won't do a thing unless you and I both agree that it's safe and a good thing to do.'

He sighed, and managed a half smile. I thanked him for being courageous and willing to share his feelings with me and then asked him if he felt better about the whole thing now. He nodded his approval. 'Yeah, I'm glad you're going to be safe. Thanks, Dad.'

I waited a short while, then started the engine and drove off, feeling very glad that we'd taken the time to explore Mark's unexpressed emotions, very glad that the simple word patterns I'd learned — 'If there **was** something wrong, what might that be? If you **were** feeling something inside, what feeling might that be?' — were so effective in eliciting hidden emotion. They had helped Mark uncover and healthily express a fear that so easily could have got buried inside him.

Within minutes, Mark seemed to have returned to his normal, happy and chatty self, the issue apparently resolved. I was delighted and relieved that an innocent comment I'd made would not turn into a traumatic cell memory because of suppressed feelings. And as I drove I told Mark the story of how a hospital and its wonderful doctors and nurses had saved my life *when I had pneumonia at the age of four, knowing that his actual fear of hospitals would probably be an issue for a full Kids' Journey process at another time.*

Often, as parents, we might not know how to get through to our kids as gracefully as Kevin did with Mark. Kevin actually employed a few Journey techniques that might be useful to you.

If you noticed, Kevin mentioned how he got down to the same level that Mark was sitting. When I train the trainers for serving at Journey Intensives, I always stress how important it is when doing Journeywork to be physically at the same level as the people who are processing. Usually trainers circulate around the processing room, checking that the partners who are doing Journeywork are feeling supported and offering assistance when needed. All the trainers are instructed that when someone raises their hand for help, they are to go over to the couple working then squat or get down on their knees so that they are not towering over them and they can meet the person respectfully, eye to eye.

There's something quite intimidating about someone standing so much taller than ourselves. It can make opening up emotionally that much scarier. Remember what it was like when you were a kid? Adults seemed so big and overpowering. With children I always recommend that you physically come down to their eye-level so that the power of your physical presence doesn't overwhelm them.

Kevin also recognized how vulnerable Mark seemed, even though his head was turned away toward the window. He very sweetly *coaxed* Mark to speak the truth, coming from a soft, tender place himself. In addition to making sure we are physically on the same level as our kids, it's very important to create a safe and welcoming *atmosphere* in which they can open up. If we come at them too forcefully, we send them into retreat and they can close down and clam up. Encouraging them softly while doing Journeywork is almost always helpful. We can't force them to feel, we can only be warmly encouraging and create a safe space of open, neutral honesty free from imposed pressures.

Finally, Kevin used a variation of a word pattern that I have found particularly useful with people who are having trouble accessing or identifying their emotions. I use this word pattern with both kids and adults and somehow it acts like a key to unlocking a door we otherwise might not be able to open. It helps kids identify what they are genuinely feeling, even if they don't know for sure what that is.

The pattern is very simple, but very effective: 'I know you don't know what you're feeling, but if *you did* know, I wonder what that might be?'

That way, you are agreeing with your child that they really don't know what they are feeling, while eliciting a deeper response from their unconscious self. Sometimes this simple but potent tool can open up the most reticent of children and recalcitrant of adults.

You should feel free to use any Journeywork and its tools in any everyday situation that might occur. You'll be amazed at your child's response and the effectiveness of your easy communication.

The Immense Power
of Forgiveness

As you've been reading this book, you've undoubtedly noticed that every story includes some aspect of forgiveness – forgiveness of others, forgiveness of self, forgiveness of life. Forgiveness is an essential key in all Journey process work. It really is the precursor to all healing.

When we forgive, it's as if our hearts finally release the pain. The contraction of blame is let go of. The shame of our transgressions melts away and the iron grip of resentment and betrayal softens and dissolves. Our heart opens anew as we finally give up our stories of injustice, and true healing commences – emotionally, physically, spiritually, on all levels of being.

Forgiveness is something we do for *ourselves*. Often, we might think we are doing it for others, that we are just being altruistic, but the very instant we forgive, we feel the immediate physical result: letting go, softening and self-healing.

There is a tribe in Africa whose views on forgiveness are so whole-some that their traditions are a humbling lesson for us all. In the Babemba tribe when someone from the local village transgresses – violates one of the rules, disobeys the law or does something morally unjust – the entire village comes together to be part of the healing of that harm. The value of one human heart is so great that it requires the participation of the entire community.

Every man, woman, child and elder abandons their normal life to form a huge circle. At the centre of the circle stands the accused. First, the full account of the injustice is given; the transgression is brought to light as the perpetrator stands, figuratively speaking, naked and fully exposed to the extent of the harm done.

Then, one by one, each villager begins to reveal all the kind deeds and generous acts the accused has done in their life. They become very detailed in their descriptions of the beautiful qualities, attributes and strengths of the accused, giving specific examples and full accounts of actual events. Every good deed is recalled with great love and respect. Sometimes the ceremony goes on for *days* – however long it takes is as long as it continues. It is as if, through this ritual, the whole village is saying, 'What you *did* is *not* who you really are. Who you are is a magnificent being.'

At the end, the circle is finally broken and the one in the centre is welcomed back into the community with open arms. And a huge celebration of reunion takes place.

When we forgive, we are connecting with the truth of *who that person really is*. We recognize that though the act of transgression may not have been acceptable, still, inside, the person is a beautiful soul.

I wonder what it would be like for our children if we administered justice to them in this same enlightened way, clearly stating the wrongdoing, pointing to the unacceptable behaviour, letting them know how hurtful or damaging or dangerous their actions were, and then reminding them of their greatness.

What if we spent substantially *more time* praising them, pointing to their good traits, reminding them of their innate beauty and chronicling their good deeds? What if a part of justice included reconnecting them to the beauty of *who they really are?*

Of course I'm not suggesting that we pretend that our children's unhealthy behaviour doesn't matter. It will not serve them to gloss it over. We really do need to explain *why* the behaviour was hurtful or wrong. But then we need to let go ourselves, completely forgive and spend the largest part of our time celebrating and reconnecting them to the magnificent, shining diamond of their own soul.

I wonder how effective that might be. It might be worth giving it a try, not just with your kids, but with your spouse, parents and loved ones.

When I was little, my very wise and compassionate grandmother would often have tea with me and discuss philosophy. She firmly believed in the innate dignity of the human spirit and had no doubt that, even at a very young age, I would understand and follow her philosophical discourses. I often remember her saying, 'My dear, you must be very careful about what you look for in another human being. *You always find what you look for*; so if you look for the best in them, that is surely what you will find.'

I like to make a clear distinction between the behaviour and the person. Many times in our lifetime, actions may occur that are completely unacceptable, for instance physical abuse or violence, verbal abuse, molestation – the list goes on and on. In every culture *this sort of behaviour is totally unacceptable*. We cannot condone the behaviour. Yet in The Journey, as with the Babemba tribe, we find we can say 'No' to the behaviour and we can forgive the human soul who forgot the beauty of their own nature. We can wholly forgive the human being, while clearly saying 'No' to the actions.

When you work with your child, they will be your greatest teacher of forgiveness. They will often forgive what we ourselves are too proud or stubborn to let go of. They will often accept the simple words 'I'm sorry' innocently and sweetly, at face value, then immediately hug their friend, make up and run off to play in the sandpit as if nothing had happened. Children are naturally quick to forgive and quick to heal.

When forgiveness is truly heartfelt, genuine and free from hidden agendas, with no strings attached, it feels as if a fresh breeze wafts through our hearts. An uplift of lightness comes with our decision to let go of the pain and finish with our blame game. It's with true forgiveness that real communion and communication begin.

Sometimes it might seem that something is just not forgivable, that there is no way to let go of the hurt or find a way past the injustice. But if we are willing to let go of our own pride, willing to decide that it is more important to be kind than right, then Grace will move mountains to open our hearts and help us heal.

There is one woman whose story of forgiveness is so moving it takes my breath away. In this true account (taken from Jack Kornfield's beautiful book *The Art of Forgiveness, Lovingkindness and Peace*), one woman's largeness of heart opens all our hearts to the possibility of unconditional forgiveness:

Once on the train from Washington to Philadelphia, I found myself seated next to an African American man who worked for the State Department in India, but had quit to run a rehabilitation program for juvenile offenders in the District of Columbia. Most of the youths he worked with were gang members who had committed homicide.

One fourteen-year-old boy in his program had shot and killed an innocent teenager to prove himself to his gang. At the trial, the victim's mother sat impassively silent until the end, when the youth was convicted of the killing. After the verdict was announced, she stood up slowly and stared directly at him and stated, 'I'm going to kill you.' Then the youth was taken away to serve several years in the juvenile facility.

After the first half year the mother of the slain child went to visit his killer. He had been living on the streets before the killing, and she was the only visitor he'd had. For a time they talked, and when she left she gave him some money for cigarettes. The she started step by step to visit him more regularly, bringing food and small gifts. Near the end of his three-year sentence she asked him what he would be doing when he got out. He was confused and very uncertain, so she offered to set him up with a job at a friend's company. Then she inquired about where he would live, and since he had no family to return to, she offered him temporary use of the spare room in her home.

For eight months he lived there, ate her food, and worked at the job. Then one evening she called him into the living room to talk. She sat down opposite him and waited. Then she started,

'Do you remember in the courtroom when I said I was going to kill you?'

'I sure do,' he replied.

'Well, I did,' she went on. 'I did not want the boy who could kill my son for no reason to remain alive on this earth. I wanted him to die. That's why I started to visit you and bring you things. That's why I got you the job and let you live in my house. That's how I set about changing you. And that old boy, he's gone. So now I want to ask you, since my son is gone, and that killer is gone, if you'll stay here. I've got room, and I'd like to adopt you if you let me.' And she became the mother of her son's killer, the mother he never had.

Her story is an invitation to all of us to open our hearts to true forgiveness.

When you work with your child, you will find that often they are so quick to forgive that they might 'jump' to forgiveness, avoiding the pain of experiencing all the pent-up hurt and stored emotions, glossing over it, going straight for the easy route – out of their pain and into forgiveness. This tends not to be full or true forgiveness, but a pretence of forgiveness.

In the campfire process, you will find that there are actually two steps to forgiveness. First you empty out all the stored-up pain, and once it's all been released real forgiveness comes easily and naturally. Nature abhors a void, so when you're completely empty of all judgement, hurt, blame, anger, hatred, all the unspoken thoughts and words, when it's all been expressed and flushed out, then forgiveness rushes in to fill that void. It's as if all the love that's been hidden underneath the veils of hurt gets exposed, and then this natural love expresses itself as forgiveness.

Remember how Jade brought up forgiving the urn, without even being prompted? Once she'd vented all her upset, forgiveness and compassion became the obvious next response. So, forgiveness has two wings: letting go of the unexpressed emotion, so that it's no longer stored anywhere in our bodies, and then, from that freedom, forgiving completely and genuinely from the bottom of our hearts.

The converse is also true: if all the unexpressed emotion is not emptied out, forgiveness can feel incomplete, false or artificial. Have you ever had an argument with someone and walked away from it, vehemently saying to yourself, 'Oh, I *wish* I'd said this. If *only* I'd said that. I *should* have said blah, blah, blah ...'? Do you recognize yourself? Often these internal arguments end up getting repressed and transmuted into a deep resentment, even though we may say we're sorry to the other person. In this case forgiveness isn't real, it's what I call 'lip-service forgiveness' – we say the words, but internally we subtly hold onto our story of blame, judgement and anger. The cell memory is not fully released and the cell receptors remain closed.

So often, books on forgiveness will suggest that we repeat some form of the words 'I forgive you' as a type of affirmation, but in so doing, we never get the chance to fully face and release the stored-up emotion. The act of forgiving might feel superficially sweet, but when we scratch the surface we discover that the unaddressed hurt and blame are still boiling underneath. Then, the next time we have an argument with that person, the stuffed resentment and stored anger come up again, only this time louder, stronger and pissed off that we didn't express the truth first time.

Have you ever had the *opposite* experience? Where you have an argument, walk away from it, start talking to yourself and then stop and say to yourself, 'I'm not holding it back this time. I'm going to face that person and let them know how hurt I really am.' Have you noticed what happens when you empty out and share your true feelings and heartfelt pain? Inevitably, the other person senses your vulnerability and feels they can share the truth of how they are feeling, and when you are both completely and utterly empty, forgiveness arises naturally and fully, seemingly out of nowhere. You kiss and make up.

These are the arguments that *don't* get stored in our bodies: they burn a clean ash. When true forgiveness has taken place, it should feel as if it's swept your heart clean, like a fresh breeze has blown through. Then the story of pain is completely over. However, if there is any holding back, keeping score or 'gunny sacking', then forgiveness feels unsatisfying, incomplete, even phoney. It's partial forgiveness at best, and it leaves a messy aftermath.

So, when working with your kids, it's essential to encourage them to *really release and empty out their stored-up feelings at the campfire*. Once they are empty they will spontaneously *want* to forgive. And true healing begins with the wholehearted for-giveness.

My journey started when I walked down the stairs and felt my source, it felt like when I'm playing with my dog or in a nice hot bath. My mentor was Jesus because I can trust him. When I was in the rocket I went to the eye because that's where your tears come from and I wanted to stop them at the end. I felt really sad and alone. I've felt like this when my brother has hurt me and nobody did anything to see if I was ok. At the campfire, my mum and dad were there and I asked them why they didn't ask me if I was OK then they said because you're old enough now and Daniel (my brother) doesn't know what he's doing because he's only 4. So I forgave them and they said they were sorry. The balloons to help the movie change were strength and courage. The body changed and the tears stopped falling from my eyes. My trip home was great and I felt much better.

Siobhan

8

Divorce and Relationship Issues

Divorce is an issue that will unfortunately affect nearly one out of every two families. It is probably the most common issue you will encounter when working with children, and yet it's a process for which there is not just one easy answer.

I call divorce a process because unlike the death of a loved one, which can occur unexpectedly, in a single day, separation and divorce usually take place over the course of several months, and if particularly litigious can even drag on for years.

Even if we are extremely conscientious with our children, consciously trying to keep the situation as healthy, open and honest as possible, our children are bound to have all kinds of unspoken emotions about the loss of the family as a single unit. They often feel responsible and/or helpless. They will try to figure out who is to blame and how they can fix things. They will internalize their hurt, and often that can get transmuted into behaviour that is angry, withdrawn, hostile, hurtful or even self-damaging.

There are such a wide variety of responses, and none of us were given the manual 'How to Handle the Pain of Separation, Loss and Estrangement'. We tend to keep our hurts to ourselves and our judgements in our heads, yet our pain leaks out sometimes at the most unexpected moments, in inappropriate ways. Undoubtedly, if you are separated or divorced, your child will have some private unaddressed issues. Generally speaking, it's not just one issue but several that get stored up, and it usually takes more than one Kids' Journey to unearth and heal the myriad hurts.

As a matter of fact, if there has been a divorce, *I recommend that your child has multiple kids' processes*. Undoubtedly, over the course of the several months of often painful arguments, our children will have internalized much of the pain, and their unasked questions need healthy answers. Your child will need private and anonymous ways of releasing all that pain and experiencing all the blame and judgement, and will need time to forgive you as well as themselves. They will need to find true understanding in order to come to a place of acceptance, peace and wholeness around this subject.

When it comes to Kids' Journeys, I always suggest that your child experiences their first few processes with a dear friend, a relation or a therapist rather than a parent. In the case of divorce, I feel it's not just preferable, *it's essential*.

Very often children will open up to strangers or distant relatives when they know that the content of their process will be kept entirely confidential. They will express feelings that they would never dare to share with their parents. They will feel safe to express their anger and their hurt, find their own answers and come to a place of forgiveness if we're not around to judge or monitor them. So I'd like to *strongly* recommend that you find them a favourite aunt, uncle, friend or therapist you can trust, so they can feel the same safety that we require when we undergo our own healing process work.

Children deserve the same anonymity that we need. This is true in even the healthiest of divorces.

Recently, a dear friend of ours who is a single mum asked for her daughter Emma to have a private Kids' Journey with a Journey Accredited Therapist. Emma, who is nine going on nineteen, is bright, open, expressive and independent. And to watch Maddie and Emma together is to witness the warmest of mother/daughter relationships. You would definitely classify their relationship as a healthy and happy one, one that we would all want to model.

Each Christmas is a very poignant time for them because, on Boxing Day, Emma flies off to spend time with her beloved dad on the other side of Australia. Emma openly loves her father, and

Maddie encourages her to spend this precious six-week period with her dad. All year long Emma looks forward with great anticipation to her special time with her father, and yet when Maddie and Emma see each other off at the airport, it's always a heart-rending and tearful parting. Their love is so strong and they are so close that six weeks seems like a lifetime for the pair.

Maddie knows her daughter well and kept saying that even though Emma seemed so well-adjusted, she still had unresolved issues around the divorce. She knew, in spite of their closeness, that she was definitely *not* the one to partner Emma in her Kids' Journey – in fact Emma also *insisted* that she didn't! So Maddie called The Journey office and arranged for Emma to choose which therapist to work with.

Emma has kindly consented to us telling her story here, so that all parents can be inspired to support their kids in going on their own private Journeys, and Suzi, the Accredited Therapist who partnered her, has kindly written up Emma's story.

> During the process, Emma finally went back to the time of the divorce. During that time she'd felt unable to express herself and stymied in sharing her pain. So, at her campfire everything came flooding out at once: all the unexpressed words, thoughts, judgements and hurt. The younger Emma began to plead with

both her parents, begging them not to break up. She'd never had a chance to plead her case before and she'd always wanted to ask what she could do to get her parents to like each other again.

*She desperately needed to release all these pent-up unspoken words from that old memory. Then she expressed **huge** amounts of rage; so much so that she admitted to wishing she could lock her mother in prison! In all this there was a feeling of helplessness and a fierce desire to cajole her parents into reconciliation. She desperately wanted to broker a deal – not an uncommon prayer for kids of divorce.*

*Once Emma had been allowed to completely empty out all her helpless desperation and rage, both parents were finally given a chance to speak at the campfire. They both explained their situation, which Emma found **very** helpful, and after speaking to her mentor (her white cat, Kabir, who happens to be an angel in disguise!) she decided on her own that it was good seeing her father on holidays, because it was 'special time', and she could have loads of one-on-one quality time with him that other kids with dads at home often didn't seem to have. Her father explained to her that even though he couldn't live with her, he loved her very deeply. He also said that he loved her mother – they just couldn't live together.*

After an exhaustive session letting go of years of stored pain, Emma was finally able to completely forgive her dad with all her heart. When it came to her mum, she found forgiveness didn't come so easily. More rage and anger needed to come out. It often happens that children will blame the parent that they live with, while idolizing the other parent from afar. This was definitely the case with Emma.

When it was time to forgive her mum, Emma wasn't sure it was 100 per cent real, so she asked her mentor what she should do next. Kabir suggested that Emma might want to step inside her mum to feel what her mother was going through emotionally at the time of the divorce. When Emma went inside her mum, she was shocked to find there was a garden there that was very barren and filled with weeds. She could palpably feel her mother's loneliness and confusion. Emma felt great compassion for her mum and spontaneously came up with a viable solution. She went into her own heart, where there was a rose garden, full of flowers in full bloom, and she picked a beautiful rose from her own heart and gave it to her mother.

In her simple, child-like manner, she was expressing her love and forgiveness to her heartbroken mum.

Towards the end of the campfire Emma said to Suzi that of

*course she couldn't give her mum the **actual** rose from her heart because it was only imaginary. Suzi asked, 'Well, what could you do in **real** life?' and Emma came up with the perfect solution: she could draw a picture of a rose garden and give that tangible gift to her mum as an expression of her love.*

*Whilst still at the campfire, Suzi asked, 'Why don't you imagine giving her that picture **now** and then go inside her again and see how she responds?' When Emma went back inside Maddie, in place of the barren garden with weeds there was now a beautiful rose garden full of new growth and fresh flowers. When Suzi asked Kabir what inner qualities were in the garden, Emma replied that love and understanding had taken the place of loneliness and confusion.*

Emma was literally going about the process of letting go of her own pain, forgiving and then helping her parents heal *their* pain!

Children so want to heal, and their natural goodness is so generous that they long to bring that same healing to us as well.

When her process was over, Emma was looking much more relaxed, at ease and at peace, yet she had the wisdom to admit to Suzi that she really needed a couple more Journeys just to make sure all the issues from that time were fully cleared out.

I've subsequently heard that this past Christmas Emma gave her mother not just one picture, but *all* the artwork she had painted during the whole year – an *abundance* of love expressed through her art. Emma is a beautiful example of just how much we are able to let go of when we feel safe in the privacy offered by a neutral support person. And she reminds us all that there are often many facets to healing from the pain caused by divorce.

When there has been a particularly messy relationship between mums and dads, it can sometimes happen that the child will internalize their anger and blame to such an unhealthy degree that it ends up being expressed as defiance, delinquency and anti-social behaviour, and the child can even turn to drugs and violence.

Jayshree, the remarkably caring teacher I wrote about in an earlier chapter, sent me a case study of one such child. Mandla was a defiant, hostile and sometimes violent 14 year old who had flunked out of school so many times that he still had to do primary-school classes with ten-year-old kids. He was hauled up so frequently for delinquency that the tribal elder in his community beat him regularly for his transgressions – an accepted practice within the tribe. He was also brutally beaten by the local police on many occasions. Ultimately, Mandla ended up joining a violent gang and started glue-sniffing and stealing.

In desperation his mother Vusi, a janitor at the local school, turned to locking him up at home to keep him from further deviance, but nothing seemed to get through to him. He wore his steely defiance like cold armour. He couldn't care less. He hated the authorities, teachers and all adults, including his parents. He hated life. Not an easy nut to crack.

Jayshree felt deep compassion for the troubled teenager, though there was no hope of helping him in the 'normal' way with his studies. She had no clue as to what was troubling him, but one day was able to persuade him to do a private Journey process with her. Over the next few weeks she did three more with him.

During these processes the whole pattern began to unfold as Mandla peeled back the layers. When he was a young child his father had many affairs and several illegitimate children. It seemed to young Mandla that all these other kids, who weren't even his 'real' brothers and sisters, got all the attention and love that he should have been getting, and he felt furious, robbed and betrayed by his dad. Somehow he was able to hold it all together because his mum was a 'saint' through everything. She was a model of goodness, and though his father could not be forgiven, at least his mum knew what was right and wrong. It gave him hope that there was some good left in the world and some semblance of stability in his otherwise hopeless and unstable family life. Then, when he was ten years old, it all fell apart. His fed-up mother had an affair and Mandla's whole world came tumbling down around him.

If even his saintly mother didn't do what was right and good, Mandla thought it must mean that there was no good left in the world. If his parents weren't subject to rules of right and wrong and simple decency, then no rules applied to him. From that moment onwards he said a big 'Fuck it!' to the world. 'There's no such thing as right and wrong, there's no good left any more, so why even bother?'

As the rules didn't apply to him, why even bother going to school, let alone doing homework? Instead he decided to live a life outside the rules of society. Of course it seemed natural to fall in with other lawless kids who'd given up on any goodness. They were the only ones who understood that rules didn't mean anything.

During his Journey process, Mandla finally let go of all his heartbreaking rage and anger at his dad. He screamed out his fury at having 'bastard' brothers and sisters and emptied out his secret hurt that he never felt loved or specially treated as his father's only legitimate son. He railed at his mother and at how his world had caved in when she had the affair and he didn't even know what was right or wrong any more. He had been too angry to care.

Somehow, once Mandla was empty, he came to understand at 14 what he couldn't understand at 10: how much pain his mum had been in, how unloved *she* had felt, how betrayed and hurt she had been, and how much she'd covered up for his sake. He understood her love for him and realized that her pain was much like his own. He was finally able to forgive his mum, and in that forgiveness, a little light began to come through a crack in his armoured defiance.

Three processes and six months later, Mandla was a model student. Jayshree says that now he finishes all his homework and has moved up a grade in school. His mother says he's become so considerate that he even took a part-time job in order to buy her a Mother's Day gift. He's no longer a gang member, his glue-sniffing has stopped and the natural goodness that he always had as a young boy has begun to shine through again. Jayshree helped him lift the hardened lampshade off his light.

Jayshree sent me this beautiful letter from Mandla's mother Vusi:

My son was joining all the 'squotens', i.e. the school dropouts and the delinquents who sniffed glue and went on the rampage stealing from squatters [informal settlements much like ghettos]. At times he would disappear for two weeks and then come home riddled with skin diseases, with a bleeding nose from glue-sniffing, and zombie-like. He did not want to go to school at all. He had failed three times already and was too big for his grade. He never did any homework and refused any oral test as well. I gave up and asked my fellow janitor at the school to whip him every day. This did not work as he still ran away, came back, was whipped, ran away … I could not take it anymore!

Finally I decided to call the police and lock him up! But God saved us all, as Mandla my boy landed in a good teacher's class who asked me not to whip him or call the police. I really thought that this teacher was mad! How could she help somebody like Mandla when all else had failed? She asked for a little time to help him and I said yes.

Jesus! That teacher, she did magic! She explained that it is The Journey, but I still call it magic! She sat with him for a few minutes every day and helped him with things that he saw in his mind and it was shocking! My Mandla changed overnight! He began liking the school, having better friends and laughing and playing. It was Mother's Day and my boy went out in the village and he carried groceries to the cars and got R20-00. He came home and said, 'Ma, this is for you ... Happy Mother's Day! I will also make you a cup of tea!'

*'This is my Mandla!' I cried. 'My **real** Mandla. Thank you, Jesus! Thank you, Journey magic! Thank you, Ma Mannie!'*

Mandla has passed Grade 5 and is very happy. We are all very happy. Mandla says if he has lots of money he will one day buy his teacher many gifts! He likes her so much! Me too! He is doing OK at school and finishing homework and working hard. My boy, he is so good now!

Vusi's very raw and heartfelt letter speaks volumes to every parent's heart and is a testament that even in the most dire-seeming circumstances, our children can rediscover their true goodness. Their story gives all of us hope for true healing and forgiveness.

The stories of healing from divorce and relationship issues are so myriad and diverse, I could write an entire book on them and still not do more than scratch the surface. Yet, in each case, multiple

Journey processes helped to free these young kids from their layers of pain. They are examples to us of the depth of reconciliation and healing that is available to all humanity.

Dear Brandon and Kevin

I would like to thank you for the Journey work, which you have created. It has changed my life.

It has changed my life by me now realizing a lot of stuff I didn't realize before. Things like my Mum does actually love me, because before the Journey work I wasn't sure. I had things in my head, like my Dad didn't want to see me (because he left when I was 4). I realize now that he just wasn't ready yet to have a relationship with me and that he does love me.

Because I once believed before Journey work that he didn't love me, I used to feel unwanted and unloved. This affected my behaviour, as I was always trying to get other people's attention at home and at school. For instance, at school I took my anger out on teachers and in lessons I used to always get out of my seat so they'd notice me. Whenever anyone talked about going to see their Dad, this made me feel lonely.

I was always in trouble at school. I broke the record for being on a pastoral support programme (for naughty kids) longer than anyone else in the school. Since Journey work, not only am I not on a PSP, I have no complaints from any teacher.

At home, since Mum has heard about my Journey work, she has felt more about me. She has said things like, 'Warren, I am so proud of you,' which she never said before. In fact, she is so proud and happy for me, she went out and bought me loads of computer games.

I feel better with my Mum and closer to her. I think Journey work should be used in all schools, because it has made such a difference to my life.

Can I thank you again for doing this, as my life is now worthwhile.

Best wishes,
Warren

9

Empowering Internal Resources

In the earlier chapters, through each of the children's inspiring stories, we've been learning how The Journey works in real life. We've been discovering specific tools that are part of every successful Journey; we've learned about the magical steps that carry us into the presence of love inside, and we've learned about the imaginary mentor who can give us access to our own deep inner wisdom. We have taken the special space shuttle into the body to access specific cell memories, and once we're at the campfire, we've learned how important it is to express, release *and* forgive the stored emotions from the old memory. We've discovered the healing power of true heartfelt forgiveness and found out how our own inner mentor can give us answers to questions that have never been answered. Ultimately, we've learned that it is possible to free our own potential and that our bodies are capable of healing naturally. We've realized how important it is to clear out the past and open ourselves to our own wholeness, genius, love, creativity and joy.

One very important aspect of The Journey process involves programming our cells positively and wholesomely, so that in future we can respond to stressful situations from a healthier place. We can programme in empowering, resourceful qualities that allow us to respond wholesomely to a variety of possible future scenarios.

Our healing brain works much like a computer. It will run our old programming on automatic pilot, always going the same route, playing the same unresourceful patterns again and again, *unless* we give it *new* software. If we give the healing brain healthier, more resourceful options, when it gets to the point of choice between the old unhealthy way or the new, more elegant and healthy programming, *it will always choose the most resourceful programming available*. If new resourceful programming is available, then that is what our healing brains will choose.

So, in the Change Memory process, we see how we *would have* responded more healthily in the old cell memory if we had had empowering resources available to us, and we also set it up so that in future, if the situation arises again, we will respond wholesomely.

In the Change Memory process, once we have access to the full memory that has been stored in our cells, we put it up onto a video screen and to begin with we let it go blank, knowing we can have access to it in a moment. Then the younger you from that scene steps down off the screen, comes over to the campfire and receives balloons from the mentor. Stored inside each balloon is an internal quality or empowering resource that *would* have been useful at the time of the memory; qualities like self-worth, self-confidence, love, courage, the ability to express ourselves, fun, creativity in our communication, a sense of humour, a crystal dome (so that all criticism rolls off), understanding, wisdom, etc., etc.

So, for instance, if it's a scene where Daddy is yelling, we might receive a balloon of understanding that he's just in a bad mood, another of self-love and another of creativity in communication (so that we can speak to Daddy at another time, when he is more receptive). We might receive a balloon of looking for love in the *right* places – to get love from people or pets who *can* give it healthily at that moment. Perhaps we might receive a balloon of knowing that Daddy really loves us and that he's just hurting, and we'd definitely get a balloon of a crystal dome, which allows all criticism born of Daddy's own hurt to roll off, while letting Daddy's love come through.

With each balloon, we breathe in the quality, let it suffuse our whole body and fill our entire being. Then, with all these helpful and wholesome resources, we step back onto the screen and actually play the scene the way it *would have happened* if we had had all those internal qualities at the time.

So in this case, you'd still see Daddy yelling, only you'd feel full of love and you'd understand that he was just in a bad mood. His criticism wouldn't touch you, it would just roll off, and you'd find Daddy at a later time, when he was in a better mood, and you'd express what came up for you. In the meantime, you'd go play with your dog or friends, and rest in your own presence of self-love.

So, first you'd see the scene the unhealthy way and then, once you'd received your resource balloons, you'd experience it the healthy, joyous and free way.

Once your brain has experienced that healthier way, *if* the situation was ever to reoccur in the *future*, your brain and body would know how to respond wholesomely. Remember, *your brain will always choose the healthiest programming available*. So, even though the Change Memory process cannot change your past, it most definitely *can* empower you to respond more healthily in the future.

Though the Change Memory process is a simple and joyful one, it is immensely powerful. It ultimately empowers us and our kids to know that we can respond joyously and freely in future situations. One mother wrote us an inspiring account of how her child used her resource balloons to realize her long-held dream of winning a role in a stage musical:

> *My nine-year-old daughter Alana sings and dances, and her goal or her 'dream' has been to be in a stage musical.We did lots of Journeys throughout the year in which she gave herself balloons of confidence, courage, belief in herself, trust, faith and many more — these were the major ones. She went for a couple of auditions where over 1,000 kids auditioned, didn't get through, and in subsequent Journeys gave herself balloons of never giving up ('persistence' in her words), and learning from her experiences.When she imagined herself in future scenes, she could see herself on stage, confident, singing and dancing, and she knew that she had a gift of uplifting and bringing joy to people through her performance. She saw it, visualized it, knew it, future paced it. The power of absolute belief in herself — no conscious critical awareness!*

> *Then a newspaper advertisement by a well-known amateur theatre company called for kids to audition for **The Sound of Music**. Over 365 kids auditioned, and she auditioned for the part of Marta, the second youngest Von Trapp girl. Twenty-five kids were called back, out of which the company required 12 children — two casts of six to play the youngest kids. Alana was one of the 25.*

In the car on the way to the audition she was tired, and every time she practised her singing it was as if something was stuck in her throat. I got her to close her eyes and took her down the stairs into what was an 'abridged version Journey'. I improvised a 'healing crystal' resource that spun round in her throat, clearing the debris so that the throat was open and vast, and gave her a nightingale voice balloon, so she could sing freely.

*She opened her eyes, felt refreshed, was able to sing beautifully **and got the part!** She begins rehearsals in February, and the play will run in May. Alana is probably the most empowered and confident child in her class, and she uses The Journey process to help her friends with their problems. It just brings back home to me how easy it is for our kids to empower themselves. They are so accepting, so open, and it's easy to teach them at such an early age that they create their own life!*

Resource balloons can definitely have a hugely empowering effect on our kids' confidence and ability for future events.

As you know, the Kids' Journey is currently used in kids' programmes in abuse centres and in addiction programmes. One particular Accredited Therapist, Angie, has been doing exceptionally beautiful work with a youth programme in Soweto, South Africa.

Part of the vision for the youth group is to empower the teenagers to recognize their own innate dignity and self-worth, so that they will choose to stay off drugs and will refuse to let their bodies be sexually or physically abused. Each of the kids has undergone multiple Journeys, and they are such a joy to meet. In addition to Journeys, they learn to perform music and dance indigenous to their culture, and I recently invited the entire group to join us at an adult Journey Intensive in Johannesburg. Not only were the teenagers models of self-confidence, inner beauty and joy, but they also enchanted us with a concert of song and dance that was so heartfelt there was barely a dry eye left in the room.

There are some balloons that we as therapists have found particularly useful in the case of physical, sexual and verbal abuse. Even though we can't undo the past, we *can* help give our young people some internal resources that will support them strongly in the future.

When it comes to sexual abuse, very often the child will feel as if they've been 'stained for life' – as if there's a stain that just can't be rubbed out. We have found it very useful to give the child a balloon of realizing that their *soul* is a radiant diamond – pristine, flawless and pure. We help them to understand that throughout our life, though horrible things happen to our bodies (for example, as we get older catheters and all kinds of tubes might end up attached to our physical forms), the flawless purity and radiance of our essence are *untouched* by what takes place with our form, so a balloon of purity that's untouched by negative physical events is always helpful.

We also find that in the case of bullying it is sometimes useful to have a balloon with the courage to say 'no'. Sometimes, creativity in communication might be useful – water pistols, dropping a water balloon, tickling, screaming and laughing can all be useful in interrupting a negative pattern. Sometimes what is needed is the ability to ask for help. Very often, schoolkids don't know that there are organizations that can help in such instances, or that they can go to their teacher, school counsellor, mum or dad.

In the case of verbal abuse, a crystal dome is almost always useful. The clear dome lets all the harsh, hurtful words roll off while the child sits comfortably inside the dome, resting in peace. Only the energy of love can penetrate through the pores of the dome. Coupled with the crystal dome is the recognition that when someone says something mean or hurtful it's because that person is in some sort of pain, and they are just acting out their distorted and unresolved issues. Compassion is also useful at such a time.

A Source balloon is always useful in just about *any* situation. Knowing that our true essence is a diamond, a presence of love, peace and joy, can only help.

Wisdom to see the larger picture is also often useful. Remember Mandla's story, how he could understand at 14 that his mum was feeling pain similar to his own, something that he hadn't understood at the age of 10?

Sometimes a child needs a balloon that might seem obvious to us, but not so obvious to the child. 'Looking for love in the *right* places' can be a very useful balloon. Often, as parents, we may have metaphorically put a 'Do Not Disturb' sign on our doors when we are under some sort of stress. In a case like this, it's as if your child has blinkers on; they have tunnel vision, and the only place they think they could possibly find love is from their parents. What might be more helpful for that child, at that particular moment, would be to take the blinkers off, turn around and face the rest of the world. There are a few billion people out there, and perhaps a few of the closer ones might be able to give love healthily at that moment. Perhaps even a dog or a teddy bear or a neighbour's mum could give the nourishment needed. So looking for love from people who *can* give it healthily at that moment is a good resource.

Most kids will want a sense of humour balloon. I think we all understand that life would be much easier if we didn't take ourselves so seriously and others so personally. And I always throw in a self-worth and self-confidence balloon. I can think of no circumstance when those qualities aren't useful.

As you work with your kids (and your adult friends), you will find that the perfect balloon qualities will start popping up spontaneously as you relax with the processes. It's good to first ask your child what they think would be useful, and if they run out of options it's kind to throw in a few extra suggestions for good measure. Over time you'll find that more and more creative balloons will arise, seemingly out of nowhere. Remember when Alana's mother gave her the vibrating crystal that cleared her throat and a balloon that made her sing like a nightingale? Though neither of these qualities are among the 'standards' or classics used, they were nonetheless highly creative and entirely appropriate for the situation. So I hope you will be inspired to give your children's and your own creativity full rein.

Perhaps you've heard the expression 'Less is more'? Well, in the case of balloons, less is *not* more. *More* is more! So be abundant in your choice of internal resources.

10

And the Greatest of
These is Love …

When all is said and done, the greatest and most healing gift you have is the one you brought with you when you picked up this book: the immense power of your own love for your child. No process, tool or technique could possibly match your love, adoration and praise. Indeed, the processes in this book only come alive through the magically transformative energy of your love. True healing begins in the embrace of love you provide for your child, and it's something no one else can do for you. It can only arise from your own heart.

I pray we never underestimate how deeply our love penetrates, or how effective it is in uplifting and healing just about *any* situation.

I recently read in a science magazine that quantum physicists have to perform double-blind experiments as they have found that the thoughts and expectations of the scientists doing the tests are affecting the physical outcome of the research. It's amazing to contemplate that science can actually observe the effect our thoughts have on quantifiable results. It all sounded like a fantastical notion until I had a direct experience of this sort of thing myself.

About a year ago, I had an experience of love that really stunned me and forever changed my perspective on the immense *power* of its healing force. I was given a beautiful bouquet of white lilies and cream-coloured long-stemmed roses. I cut the stems and placed them in fresh water, and for several days the flowers bloomed to absolute fullness. They were just *bursting* with life. Then one morning, on my way to a seminar, I put them on a table in the shade on my deck, thinking they might enjoy the cool autumn air. Later that day, when I arrived home, I discovered that the vase had toppled over and all the water had run out. My fabulous lilies looked drooped and faded, the edges were brown and the petals were falling off. The roses had dropped their heads entirely. Quickly, I rushed into the house, cut their stems and placed them back in fresh water, half-heartedly hoping it might somehow refresh them. Having been a flower lover since a young child, I was very accustomed to their cycles, and I didn't hold out much hope that they would actually come back to life, but it could never hurt to try.

The next morning when I rose my poor lilies looked completely lifeless, unable to draw upon the water, and the roses were bent over with dropped heads that signalled to me that there wasn't really much life-force left. I'd never seen a rose raise its head once it had grown heavy and fully dropped. Sadly, I realized that when I came home that afternoon I would have to throw out the whole bouquet as it would only begin to stink.

As I looked at the blooms, I suddenly felt touched by their fragile beauty. I realized what glorious expressions of nature they were. I sat down with them and, internally, began to thank them for the loveliness they had brought over the last few days. I praised their exquisiteness and admired their tiny striations and the nuances of hue. I got lost in a reverie of gratitude that such exquisiteness should be allowed to come before my eyes.

As I turned to go off to work, I got a lump in my throat that such tender sweetness should be so short-lived and fragile. As I left the house, I felt full; grateful that I'd taken the time to cherish and savour the flowers' last moments of life.

Later that afternoon, I came home and beheld what to me seemed a miracle. The roses had somehow lifted their heavy heads and were standing proud and exalted in their own sensuous beauty. And the lilies had come out of their slump, and though the brown edges were still there, they were standing strong, vibrant and bursting with life! It wasn't possible, but there it was.

I stood there stunned, awed. I'd loved flowers all my life, I always had at least one fresh bunch on my dining table, and yet in all these years I'd never seen a rose raise its head or a faded lily come back to life.

The flowers continued to bloom exaltedly for another five days. I brought friends and neighbours round to view their amazing grace. All were touched.

If a few moments of unabashed praise and adoration can bring a flower back to life, what can it do for our kids? Our children are just like these flowers – they come to life, burst with amazing grace, when we take time to stop and honour and adore them. When we embrace them in our love, their potential blooms, their soul shines.

I recently shared this story with a dear friend who has two beautiful sons. She said, 'Brandon, I feel all parents intrinsically understand the power of praise. We see it clearly. What I've found particularly useful is not just praising my kids as a matter of course. All children can feel the difference between an absent-minded, carelessly tossed out "Well done" or "Good job" and specific and carefully thought-out praise. I always take a moment to be present to my child and to really look at, say, his drawing. I find something specific that is particularly praiseworthy, and I point that out.

When he plays cricket I remember the one move that was particularly good, or I comment on how extraordinarily imaginative he is in his character portrayal in a story he has written. I notice how much he glows when I offer true, heartfelt praise. It only takes a moment, but I see his confidence growing right before my eyes.'

We truly can become gardeners in our children's lives. Our love is the very water they drink, the air they breathe, and with the Journey process we weed out any stifling weeds. We till the soil, giving lots of room for their tender roots to grow, and in the shining presence of our light, our children flourish and bloom with such vibrancy that their radiance takes our breath away.

Our love creates the embrace that breathes life into these beautiful souls.

Indeed, of all our gifts, 'The greatest of these is love.'

PART
TWO

A Healing
Adventure for Kids

Working with Little Ones with a Magical and
Therapeutic Bedtime Story

11

A Healing Adventure for Kids: Instructions

I've written this Healing Adventure specifically for five to seven year olds. In offering the Junior Journey workshops, we noticed that when little ones got to the full unabridged Kids' Journey they were often too antsy and restless, too fidgety to sit through the entire process. So we had to get creative and find a joyous, yet effective way for them to process that would both engage and enchant them.

'A Healing Adventure for Kids' was born to meet that challenge. This magical adventure or bedtime story – full of fun and complete with pictures – can be read like a fairytale in much the same way that you would read a normal bedtime story to your child.

What makes this fairytale so special is that it is written as a 'therapeutic metaphor', designed to reach your child at a deep subliminal level and to catalyse healing. Dr Milton Erickson, one of the most famous medical psychologists of the last century, was best known for telling his patients magical stories that effected emotional and physical healing. His powerfully transformative linguistic techniques have become widely known as 'therapeutic metaphors'. While his patients were rapt, listening to his beautiful stories, the words reached deeply into the other-than-conscious, to the 'healing brain', to awaken and promote natural healing. His results were remarkable.

So 'A Healing Adventure for Kids' is a joyous, healing and natural way for you to work with your child. Rather than overtly going through an actual campfire process, it is suggesting to the healing brain that it is already taking place. Every sentence in the Healing Adventure is designed to leave your child in a positive, healthful place, so even if they drop off to sleep mid-story, they will still feel surrounded by light and filled with a presence of love. The process is joyous, gentle and fun. And if your child *wants* to actively participate and do the process out loud, the wording also allows for that kind of full participation. Otherwise they can just relax and let it all happen at an other-than-conscious level, like playing make-believe. Either way, passive or active, the Healing Adventure will have positive results.

As you already know, the more you enliven the details of a story and bring them to life, the more enchanted your child feels. I certainly don't need to tell you how to be lively and playful with your child – you've undoubtedly learned by now that in order to play with a child, you have to become one.

Before you start, I strongly recommend you read all of Part 1 of this book. That way, you will fully understand the various steps of the process and in time you can become quite creative in your use of the process work.

Although I have designed this adventure story for five to seven year olds, I also recommend that eight to twelve year olds either read it themselves or have it read or explained fully to them. In this way they will fully understand the process *ahead of time* and when they come to do the full Kids' Journey that is designed for their age group they can just relax and enjoy actively participating in the process.

As your five to seven year olds really get used to the Healing Adventure, and when you feel they are ready, you can move on to a condensed version of the older Kids' Journey (*see Part 3*). It's something that will likely happen naturally, and often comes about spontaneously as they get more and more facile with the work. Once children move on to the full Kids' Journey, as already mentioned, I recommend they get their first few processes with someone other than their parent – maybe a friend, aunt, uncle or therapist. In the beginning, it often turns out that we, the parents, are the ones kids process with at the campfire, and they will require the same anonymity in their process work that you and I would expect in ours.

Kids *love, love, love* The Journey and take to it with great gusto. There is likely to come a time when they will start helping *their* friends by doing Journey processes with them, and they may also spontaneously do them on their own before they go to sleep at night.

Before you start, a couple of tips:

> *When it comes to resource balloons, make sure you get really creative and inventive and give the kids loads. Remember, more really is* **more**.

> *Have fun, play and trust yourself. You may be surprised that as you are processing with your kids, your own issues might start clearing, and your body might even start to heal. Most of all, know that as you have fun, your kids will have fun too.*

 **Happy Journeys!**

12

A Healing Adventure for Kids

Once upon a time there was a little boy named Jamie and one night as he was drifting off to sleep he began to dream a very special dream. As a matter of fact, he wasn't even sure if he was really awake or really asleep, but somehow it was like lying in a cloud of peace, surrounded by love.

In front of him there appeared a very special downward-facing staircase that had 10 magical, sparkling steps and Jamie wondered what would happen if he stepped onto them. Feeling surrounded by love, somehow he just knew that if he stepped onto these steps he'd be carried off on an exciting adventure. So with a little excitement and some gleeful, fun-like curiosity, he ventured onto step 10 – the top step.

I wonder what colour that step is? Can you imagine what it must be like to step onto that step? What if you were to join Jamie on his Journey now? … Stepping onto step number 10 … then down one step, to step number 9 ... then 8.

Jamie began to notice that as he slowly stepped onto each step, he could feel his energy grow and grow with each step he took! He noticed with excitement how light he was feeling as he stepped onto step 7, and he felt himself beginning to relax now, and almost felt that he was floating. He stepped onto step 6 as his energy grew even larger and he grew even lighter as he stepped onto 5. Then he guessed it, 'I'm going right into the heart of the light where everything is happy, free and full of love.'

So, feeling very eager, Jamie stepped onto step 4 and then 3 as the light got brighter and brighter and the love got stronger and bigger. It almost felt like he was melting into the love – he wasn't quite sure where the love ended and he began.

'Is it on the inside of me? Is it on the outside?' he questioned ... then it began to dawn on him that the love was everywhere – inside, outside, everywhere!

Then he stepped onto step 2 and he began to feel as if he was dissolving even deeper into the light and he felt that the light sparkled with happiness. As he stepped onto step number 1 the light and love grew so big that Jamie couldn't figure out if it had any edges.

Jamie felt that he was surrounded by an ocean of light and happiness, and that love was sparkling in it everywhere. He noticed that the love and light seemed to go on and on and on forever and ever.

I wonder what that must feel like to be surrounded by love and to feel it going on and on forever and ever? How wide would it be, do you think?

While he was soaking in this ocean of sparkling love-light, a magical door suddenly appeared in front of Jamie. Jamie sensed there was something very special about this door. As a matter of fact, without knowing how he knew, he just knew that there was someone wonderful standing just behind the door, waiting for him, with welcoming arms right there in the very heart of the light. As he stood there in front of the door, he wasn't really sure who it was, but he got the feeling it was someone very, very special – maybe even an angel or a saint, a hero or a kindly wizard. He didn't know how he knew, but he just knew it was someone he felt very safe with. It was someone he could trust to protect him and safely guide him – someone who could give him good advice.

As Jamie turned the handle and stepped through the door the light was so bright he had to squint, but once his eyes had adjusted, to his great surprise right there before him was a huge smiling, glistening angel.

If you were to step through your door, I wonder who might be there waiting for you? Maybe it's an angel, or perhaps it's someone you've always wanted to meet. It must be like meeting a dear old friend.

Right away Jamie felt at home with his angel-guide and he ran over to her and gave her a big hug. Her soft angel wings surrounded them both and Jamie felt so much love and peace as she spoke her first words to him.

'Hello, Jamie,' she said. 'My name is Dorian, and I'm here to be your special guide on this wonderful inner Journey. You're totally safe with me,' she added, 'And if you've any questions, I'll be very pleased to answer them for you.'

Just as their hug finished, Jamie caught a glimpse of something shining and silver out of the corner of his eye. He turned to see what it was and, lo and behold, he realized what it was – a huge glistening space shuttle just standing there in the light with its doors wide open.

'Whoa, cool!' Jamie shouted as he tugged on the angel's sleeve, beckoning her to come and join him inside the magical space shuttle.

I wonder what it would have looked like on the outside – can you imagine? What must it be like on the inside? If you were to step inside your very own space shuttle, what might it be like?

Dorian gently folded her white angel wings so that she could fit in and sat down in the comfy seat right next to Johnny. As they buck-led their seatbelts, Dorian explained to him just how magical this vehicle was: 'It can go anywhere safely and easily inside your body. Not only that, but it knows exactly where it wants to go.'

'But where does the fuel go? What powers it?' Jamie asked.

'Oh well, that's the really magical part,' replied Dorian. 'It's powered by your own body wisdom, by the part of you that makes your heart beat and your hair grow. It's powered by the part of you that's awake when you are asleep at night, the part of you that makes your nails grow and your breath go in and out – your body wisdom. This space shuttle can take you anywhere inside your body – into your heart, your eyes, your tummy, your throat, your brain and your blood – even into your bones or muscle. Who knows where you'll end up, but because it is powered by your own body's wisdom, somehow it'll be exactly the perfect place for you to go. All you have to do is push the green button for lift-off and you'll be carried somewhere inside your body.'

Jamie wondered where he might end up, but he really didn't have a clue.

As he looked at the instrument panel in front of him, he noticed the green button for lift-off.

'When you're ready, you can push that green button and you'll be carried safely and easily inside the body,' Dorian encouraged. 'It may not be where you expect to go, Jamie, but that's part of the fun. Just push the button and you'll find yourself whizzing through the body.'

Jamie pushed it, there was a little lurch and off they went. Before he could even swallow Jamie began to feel the space shuttle gently slowing down and Dorian said, 'OK, we need to bring it in for a soft landing ... No crash landings!' Softly, it came to a stop and Jamie pulled on the handbrake.

I wonder what it might be like to ride a magical space shuttle somewhere right inside your body? What would it feel like to come in for a nice soft slow landing, and how might it feel to pull on the handbrake now?

Jamie and Dorian took off the seatbelts, and as Jamie looked down he could see there were two torches right by his feet, so he picked up one for himself, just in case there were any dark places, and handed the other to Dorian – though she was so bright, she didn't really need one!

Together they stepped outside the vehicle and it felt kind of squishy under their feet. Jamie turned on his torch and he could see exactly where they'd landed – it was inside his throat.

I wonder where you might go inside your body? What it would

feel like under your feet and what it would look like if you turned your torch on?

As Jamie and Dorian walked around, they noticed that the walls looked kind of mushy and sticky, and then they came across a place that looked somehow different from the rest of the area – it was a different colour and it had a different texture too. It even had a different temperature. I wonder what that place must be like? Can you imagine it?

To Jamie and Dorian it looked a bit scratchy, almost sandy, and they both felt curious about this spot. Holding his angel's hand,

Jamie ventured over to the rough part and put his face right up next to it, as if to feel what was there. Suddenly, a feeling of sadness, loneliness and a little scaredness seemed to come pouring off the sandy patch.

Dorian asked Jamie, 'When have you felt like this before? When have you felt this sadness and loneliness and scaredness?'

Jamie closed his eyes so he could let his mind wander. 'When have I felt like this before?' he repeated to himself inwardly. Suddenly, like magic, a picture appeared to him. It was a picture of an old memory of when he was only five years old. In his mind's eye, he looked down at his feet and noticed he was wearing the old red sandals that he used to wear on summer holidays. He'd forgotten all about those sandals, yet here they were! He looked at his legs and saw he was wearing blue shorts and his favourite red T-shirt that he'd long since outgrown. And then he remembered the whole memory. It came flooding back to him all at once.

When Jamie was five years old, he'd gone on holiday with his family to Spain. When he and his mum were shopping in an open-air market, somehow he'd forgotten to hold her hand and they had got separated and lost each other. Secretly, Jamie had felt scared, upset and so lonely. He was worried that his mum might never find him. He didn't know what to do, where to turn.

Eventually, a very kind policeman came over and talked to him until his mum finally found him. Jamie was so happy to see his mum that he didn't even let her know how scared and lonely he had been. He was afraid she might think he was a scaredy-cat or a baby or a wimp. So he pretended to her that it wasn't that big a deal, but he felt a little choked up, as though he couldn't really speak.

Once Jamie had described the whole memory to Dorian, she told him to take the memory and put it onto a videotape, knowing that he could view it another time. Then she invited him to come over to a big roaring, crackling campfire. The campfire made Jamie feel all warm and cosy inside and he noticed that the bath of love was still surrounding him. It felt so warm and safe sitting there with his beautiful loving angel, and Jamie could feel excitement building inside him because somehow he just knew there was more of this adventure to come.

If you were to sit by a warm campfire, I wonder what memory might come up for you? I wonder how old you might be in that memory and who else was there?

Jamie knew that his memory was already on the videotape and he secretly wondered what would happen to it. Then, just as he was about to ask Dorian what he should do next, she said in a kind voice, 'Jamie, it's time for you to take the videotape of that old memory and put it into the video recorder, and we'll watch it on a big movie screen in the sky.'

Jamie knew exactly what to do. He put his videotape into the slot, pressed 'play' and after a moment it suddenly appeared in living colour, right up on a huge screen in the sky. There was his old memory playing right in front of his eyes, only Jamie didn't mind seeing that old memory because he felt happy, safe and warm sitting by the toasty fire with Dorian. Besides, he knew it was just the past, just an old memory. When the scene came to an end, Dorian said something unexpected, so totally surprising that Jamie's mouth dropped and his eyes opened wide: 'Why don't you invite that younger five-year-old you to step down off the video screen and join us right here at the campfire?'

And before Jamie could close his mouth, that's exactly what happened! The five-year-old Jamie stepped down off the screen, came straight over to the fire and plonked himself down between the older Jamie and Dorian. And so now there were three of them at the campfire: the older Jamie, the younger Jamie and Dorian the angel.

If you had an old memory I wonder who'd be sitting at your campfire?

Dorian looked particularly pleased, and out of nowhere she magically produced a huge bouquet of brightly coloured balloons!

With a twinkle in her eye, she said to the younger Jamie, 'These are magical balloons! In each balloon is stored a wonderful gift – a feeling that will make you feel special all over. Stored inside these balloons are all the best qualities you need to feel good about yourself in that old memory. Which balloon do you want to choose first?'

Younger Jamie pointed to a big red balloon. 'Ah, well,' said Dorian, 'that's a very important balloon. Stored inside it is courage – all the courage you could ever need. Now take this balloon and as you hold it, breathe in the quality and let your whole body feel full of courage.'

As the younger Jamie took the balloon he could feel his whole body filling up with courage. He felt confident and happy.

'Now take this balloon,' Dorian said, as she handed him a pink balloon. 'Inside it is all the love your mum feels for you. Breathe in that love now and let it flow through every part of your body.'

As younger Jamie breathed in the love he felt all warm and glowing inside, and he realized that no matter how lost he got, he need not worry – his mum loved him so much she would always come back for him. She'd find him somehow.

'Now take this yellow balloon,' said Dorian. 'It's full of trust. Trust that if you're patient your mother will find you. Trust in life. Trust that you will be helped. Now breathe in this trust.'

Instantly, younger Jamie felt trust flooding through him and he felt safe and his body felt lighter.

Then came a green balloon. 'This is the ability to ask for help from people who can help you. Breathe in that quality.'

When he did, younger Jamie realized he didn't have anything to be ashamed of, and that it's OK to ask for help if you need to.

Then came a bright multi-coloured funny-looking balloon. 'This is a

balloon of a sense of humour and light-heartedness. It helps you realize that sometimes things happen to you, but it all works out alright in the end, and you can sometimes even enjoy it and have fun – so breathe in that quality. Now take this gold balloon – the ability to say what you're really feeling to your mum when she gets back, so you don't have to hide your true feelings anymore. So breathe that in.'

And finally Dorian gave younger Jamie a big bright blue balloon, saying, 'This wisdom balloon will help you know that all of this happened to make you wiser and stronger.' Younger Jamie breathed in the wisdom.

Dorian smiled and said, 'So with all these balloons you know that you can have courage, you can trust in Mum's love, trusting that she'll find you and that it's OK to ask for help, feeling you're safe when you ask for help, getting help and finally, when Mum returns, sharing with her how you were really feeling, knowing that sometimes these things happen in life so that we can learn how to be strong in the face of adventure and sometimes we can even have a light-hearted sense of humour while it's taking place.' Younger Jamie breathed in all the qualities and the angel said to him, 'Now in a moment you're going to step back onto the video screen and play a new scene. This time you'll play the scene the way it **would** have happened with all of your balloons.'

In an instant the five-year-old Jamie appeared back on the video screen, only this time the scene was different. There was younger Jamie holding the big bunch of brightly coloured balloons, look-ing confident and courageous. At the moment he lost his mum, he got a tiny bit scared and suddenly the courage balloon lit up as he breathed in the feeling of courage. Then the love balloon became bright, as he realized that his mum loved him and would eventu-ally find him again. Next the trust balloon became bright and Jamie knew he could relax and trust that she'd come back for him. Then the ability to ask for help balloon lit up and Jamie looked around to see if there was someone who could help him. A kind-ly policeman appeared. Jamie really liked the policeman and real-ly enjoyed talking to him – you could tell because he was smiling

and laughing as his sense of humour and light-heartedness balloon lit up. He joked with the policeman and the time just flew
by. When his mother finally found him, he told her that he had
been scared for a moment, but then he had remembered how
much she loved him, and he had trusted that she would come
back. He told her how he had tried to find help and how this kind
policeman had entertained him until she had returned. His mother sighed a big sigh of relief, thanked the policeman and hugged
Jamie. She told him how brave he was and how impressed she
was that he had waited for her and got the help he needed, and
then she added, 'You know, you weren't the only one who got
scared – I got scared too. One
moment you were there
and the next moment
you weren't! I kept
hoping that you
would be coura-
geous and wait until
I could find you, and
that you'd find help. I
love you so much! I just
couldn't wait to find you.'
As the older Jamie sat by the
warmth of the fire with his
angel, watching this whole

scene on the video screen, he realized that with the balloons that's exactly how the scene would have happened. As a matter of fact he realized that if he ever got lost again he could call upon those balloons and feel wonderful. Not only did he wish he'd always had those balloons, but he secretly wished his mum had too – because he realized she'd been just as scared as he was!

So why don't you do the same thing? Why don't you invite the younger you to step down off the video screen and come over to the warm campfire? Your guide or angel has already chosen loads and loads of balloons.

I wonder what balloons you might choose? If you could pick any you wanted, what might they be? There are so many balloons to chose from. There's love, courage, strength, wisdom, kindness, truth, honesty, self-worth, confidence, the ability to ask for help, a crystal dome that allows criticism to roll off you, a sense of humour, the ability to play and have fun, the ability to feel and to express your emotions, the ability to say 'no', a balloon of compassion, a balloon of saying you are sorry, a balloon of forgiveness, a balloon of speaking up when you're feeling shy – there's even a balloon of realizing you are full of love, and that with that love you can help others who might be scared or shy. There's a balloon of reaching out to others, and another balloon of knowing you belong. There's one that helps you know that when others are calling you names, it's just that they're feeling scared or lonely or hurt or are in a bad mood – that it's not about you. There are literally hundreds of big bright beautiful balloons to choose from. I wonder which ones you might pick now?

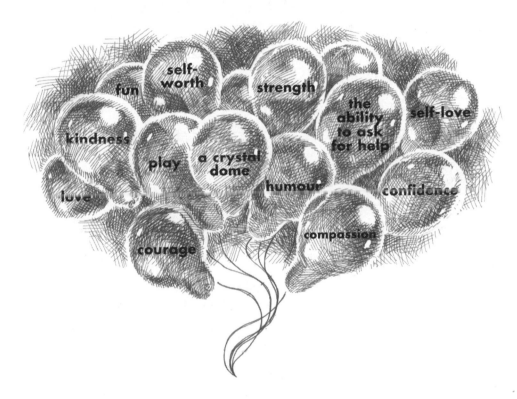

If you were to breathe in all the qualities of your balloons and let them fill up your whole body, I wonder how good that might feel? And what if you put your old memory onto a video screen in the

sky? What if you played it, this time with all your balloon qualities already inside you? I wonder how that old memory might look
now. I wonder how you might feel in it, knowing that you are full
of love, strength, courage, confidence, helping others, wisdom,
intelligence, kindness and fun – and any other qualities you've
already chosen.

If you like, you could even describe what the scene would be like
now ... and then you too, like Jamie, could step down off the
screen and sit down by a warm, cosy campfire full of love and
light. I wonder what that would be like?

For Jamie, he was amazed that he was sitting by a fire while a five-
year-old Jamie was also sitting by the same fire. He noticed how
different he looked when he was younger and he was secretly
glad he had grown up so much since then. Dorian explained to
the eight-year-old Jamie that the campfire was made of love, and
then she spoke directly to little five-year-old Jamie. She said to
him, 'You felt a lot of pain in the past, didn't you? In the real-life
memory when you got lost in the market, you got scared, you felt
alone and you didn't know where to go. You secretly worried that
your mum might not come back for you. It was a scary experience, wasn't it?'

The five-year-old Jamie nodded 'yes' as he remembered what it was really like, and a look of sadness crossed his face.

Dorian said, 'Why don't you let your mum know what you really felt like at that time? Tell her how scary it was. Get it all off your chest. Just let all those old feelings finally come out.'

Little Jamie got a tear in his eye as he said, 'Mummy, I never told you because I thought you might think I was a baby or a wimp, but I was really scared and confused. I looked and looked for you and got more and more scared when I couldn't find you. Then I began to worry that you might never come back for me. I felt so alone and so frightened.'

His mum replied, 'I was scared too, Jamie – and you know what? I didn't want you to know how scared I was. I felt frantic and desperate to find you. I love you more than life itself, and I ran back to all the places we had been to. I would run to the ends of the Earth to find you. I'm so proud of you for finding that policeman.'

Little Jamie replied, 'I'm glad you said that, Mum. I had begun to worry that you would never come back.'

'Of course I would, Jamie! You're the most precious person on Earth. I love you. If ever we get parted again, please know that I love you very much. I will always find you, I promise – just stay right where we last saw each other and wait. I will always come back.'

Little Jamie realized that his mum loved him with all her heart and he felt safe knowing she'd run to the ends of the Earth to find him – all he needed to do was stay put and trust that she would come back. He simply replied, 'Thanks, Mum.'

'I love you, Jamie,' she replied.

'I love you, Mum,' he whispered, as they hugged each other closely.

'Please forgive me for getting lost,' said Jamie.

'Of course I do, sweetie! Please forgive me for letting go of your hand. We both got lost! So we'll forgive each other!'

And they both did just that.

Dorian looked on, beaming with approval, then turned to eight-year-old Jamie and asked, 'If you had something to say to your mum now, what would you say?'

'I'd say that I really need to trust more. I needed to hear that she loves me so much that she'd go to the ends of the Earth for me. Ever since I was five I suppose I've been a little scared of being left. I never knew she loved me that much.'

'Of course I love you that much, sweetie,' replied his mum. 'With every cell of my body I love you, and I always have.'

'Thanks, Mum. I love you.'

'I'm sorry I haven't let you know more often. You mean the world to me,' his mum whispered.

'I know.'

Older Jamie and his mum gave each other a big hug.

Then Dorian said to older Jamie, 'Remember all the balloons you got earlier – the big bright ones full of wisdom, courage, trust, the ability to ask for help, the ability to express your feelings, the sense of humour, the light-heartedness balloon, the balloon filled with your mum's love? Remember them?'

As Jamie remembered them, they magically reappeared in Dorian's hand. She handed the whole bunch of balloons to older Jamie and said, 'I want you to give all these balloons to the younger you. Let him breathe them all in.'

Younger Jamie took the balloons and, as he breathed in all the qualities, his face got brighter and brighter. A big smile shone across his face and his eyes lit up with joy.

Then Dorian said to eight-year-old Jamie, 'I want you to repeat the following words to younger Jamie: "I'm so sorry you went through so much previous pain. You just didn't have access to all these beautiful inner qualities then – you didn't know that all these great strong and positive qualities are already inside you. I promise you'll never have to go through that old pain again because from now on you can have access to all of these qualities any time you like. From now on, I will take care of you."'

As older Jamie repeated the words he beamed with delight and then, out of the blue, he skipped over and hugged the younger Jamie. He whispered in his ear, 'I will always protect you. I love you.'

As he did that, something unexpected began to happen: he and his younger self began to melt right into each other. As it happened, the older Jamie began to feel all the love, joy, trust, strength, courage, wisdom and fun pour into all of his cells – into every part of his body. He realized that all the lessons he'd learned that day were becoming part of him, that every quality he had ever wanted was already part of him, that all of his words were already true and he could have access to the balloon qualities any time he liked.

Dorian was particularly pleased and said, 'Now it's time for your mum to melt into the love that's here at this campfire.'

And, as she did, everything became as bright as the sun.

Now there were just Dorian and older Jamie sitting by the fire. With a wave of her hand, Dorian made the campfire disappear and in a flash they were both back where they'd originally landed – in Jamie's throat. But now, everything looked totally different. Everything was shiny, pink and healthy looking – so bright and new. As Jamie and Dorian walked around the area, looking with their torches, they came to the place where the old rough sandy patch had been, but now it was a bright shiny area – all healed, all new and perfect in every way! It matched all the other healthy areas of the throat!

'Wow! That was like magic!' exclaimed Jamie.

'It is,' replied Dorian. 'That old memory was stored right here, in your throat. When you faced those old emotions and said how you felt and forgave, that signalled to the body to begin its healing process.'

'Cool! Can it happen that fast?'

'Of course it can – and it does all the time. Have you ever noticed how, if you cut yourself, the next day the skin is already sealed over? That's because all the cells in that area work very quickly and busily to heal it over. It works the same way *inside* your body – only faster.'

'Wow! It's so perfect, so incredible!'

'It is,' replied Dorian, with a satisfied smile. 'I wonder, if your throat could speak to you, what it might want you to know? If your throat could speak to you right now, I wonder what it might say?' Jamie cocked his head, listened carefully and suddenly heard some words come out of his throat: 'Trust that it is safe to speak out what you're feeling. Trust that your mother loves you and trust that you can express your feelings.'

Jamie listened to the words and nodded. 'I will. From now on I'm not going to choke back what I'm feeling, I'm going to feel the feeling and let my mother know – even when I'm a little scared.'

In response, the throat shone like a diamond, flashing and sparkling as if signalling its approval. It was clear that it was really pleased that Jamie had not only learned his lessons but was going to put those lessons to good use in the future. And Dorian beamed with delight.

So, if you were at your campfire right now, I wonder what you might say to the people in your memory? I wonder what they might reply? And I wonder what it would feel like to forgive them completely? And what it would feel like if they completely forgave you?

And what if the younger you received all the balloons and breathed them in? What if you hugged the younger you and felt the younger you melt into you, and felt all those amazing inner qualities fill your body? I wonder what that might feel like?

And when your campfire has disappeared, I wonder how your

body would look? I wonder if it's full of light now and looks all new and shiny? And if your body had any message for you, I wonder what it might say to you now?

Jamie felt very pleased with himself, and grateful to his body for healing so quickly now. Knowing that the healing would continue perfectly, automatically, on its own, without him even thinking about it, just like it does when you're sleeping, Jamie looked to the side of him, and there was his shiny space shuttle right there where it had originally landed.

Dorian signalled to Jamie it was time to get in and together they jumped in, strapped on their seatbelts and pushed the green button once more. Instantly, they were whisked back to the door that Jamie had first come through.

Jamie and Dorian stepped outside the shuttle. Somehow Jamie just knew that this inner adventure was over for today.

He looked up into Dorian's eyes and felt a little sad to be going.

Softly, as if she could tell how he was feeling, Dorian said, 'Jamie, I'm always here waiting inside you. Your Journey is complete for today, the healing has already begun, but you can go on another healing Journey any time you like.'

'Whoa, you're kidding! You mean I can get inside my space shuttle and explore inside my body and discover other memories there and heal them?'

'Sure! Any time you want. I'm always inside and I'll be here with your balloons, waiting until our next Journey – I can hardly wait! Until then, you have all my love.'

Dorian embraced Jamie with her soft wings and, as she did so, a little white feather fell to the ground. Jamie reached down to pick it up and by the time he stood back up Dorian had already disappeared. He heard her voice in the distance: 'I left that feather to remind you that I'm always here. Whenever you pick up a feather, know that I've sent it to you as a reminder that I'm here and that it's time to come on another inner Journey. I love you, Jamie ...'

Dorian's voice trailed off into the distance. All that remained was the tinkling sound of bells.

Jamie walked back through the doorway and saw the 10 steps he'd come down right there in front of him. He noticed how free and full of love he felt and how light his whole body felt.

He stepped onto the bottom step, step number 1, then 2, then 3 ... He could feel all the balloons and their qualities still inside him and with every step he took, they became more and more a part of him. He stepped up onto steps number 4, 5 and 6, and wondered when his next Journey might be. When he thought about how he would be in the future, he just knew that he would never choke back his feelings again – he would just feel them and share what he was feeling with his mother. He knew he was already full of courage, love, trust, kindness, wisdom and fun. With every step he took, he felt lighter and lighter, freer and freer – and so happy!

I wonder what that must feel like now?

Jamie walked up steps 7, 8 and 9, and when he stepped onto step 10, he felt very aware of the strength and love pouring through every part of his body.

Step 10. I wonder how you might feel as you step onto step number 10?

Jamie's eyes softly opened. Had he been dreaming? Was he awake? Had he imagined it all? Had it really happened? He shook his head slowly, not really sure, then turned over in his bed. Right there on his pillow was a pure white feather. He smiled as he realized that Dorian had left him a reminder, a signal that soon it would be time to go on another healing adventure. He knew Dorian would be waiting there, at the bottom of the magical steps, and, safe in this knowledge, he fell softly into a deep, peaceful sleep.

Isn't it wonderful to know that the angel is always there inside, waiting with her balloons to welcome you on another magical Journey? And what an amazing Journey it is!

PART
THREE

The Kids' Journey Process for Eight to Twelve Year Olds

13

The Kids' Journey: Instructions

Before you embark on the Kids' Journey, please read the first part of this book *thoroughly*. It offers you the teachings, subtleties, nuances, tools and skills that we have found useful over the years in working with lots of kids. Through the kids' inspiring stories you will learn of their very individual and unique ways of responding to the Kids' Journey. And once you are familiar with the skills, you will feel inspired to be creative in your use of them. So please read the first part of this book *before* proceeding.

Then, if you are planning to work with an eight- to twelve-year-old child, I recommend that you read Part 2, the younger kids' Healing Adventure. By reading it through a couple of times you will familiarize yourself with Journeywork, which forms the very basis for the older Kids' Journey process.

Once you're fully familiar with the Healing Adventure, it would be a good idea to either explain it in detail or to actually *read it out loud to your eight to twelve year old*, explaining to them that although the story is written for younger kids, they should listen to it in order to understand the principles of the work. Through listening, they will automatically absorb many of the teachings and skills and it will put their minds at ease and prepare them for their more proactively engaging Kids' Journey process. The Kids' Healing Adventure reads like a fairytale and can be a more passive experience of The Journey, whereas the full Kids' Journey process is more active, and requires the child's full participation – imaginative, verbal and emotional. So the fairytale can be a wonderfully easy way for you to prepare your eight to twelve year olds.

Then read the full Kids' Journey process a couple of times to yourself to fully familiarize yourself with the wording, the questions and responses.

Before starting, it would also be a good idea to discuss various inner resource qualities with your child-like self-worth, self-acceptance, light-heartedness, fun, play, courage, love, compassion, a crystal dome, looking for love in the right places, asking for help, the ability to say 'no', creativity in communication, the ability to reach out, and so on *(see Chapter 9 for more suggestions)*. If you discuss in advance the various internal qualities that could go in their balloons, when it comes up in their process they will have instant easy access to these healthy inner qualities.

If it is your child's first Kids' Journey, I strongly recommend that you let a kindly friend, aunt, uncle or therapist be the one to partner them. In fact, it is probably healthy for them to have this privacy for their first two or three processes. After that, they will feel so at ease with the process that they may do it on their own in bed, or with friends when playing, and they may even request that you work with them on a regular basis. One Journey dad was asked to read the Kids' Journey *every* night in place of the old fairytales he used to read!

Generally speaking, Kids' Journeys last only about 11 to 18 minutes, unless the kids are a bit older and want more thorough and expressive campfires – like Emma with the divorce issue, for example.

When reading the process you will come across '…' This indicates that it's a good place to pause and give your child sufficient time to either respond verbally or to make an internal picture. Because each child processes at their own individual pace, you'll need to be flexible with the time you allow.

In general, when working with children, it is important to be childlike and playful yourself. If you are lively and imaginative, your child will usually follow suit. Be aware that children have very quick access to their imagination and creative abilities, and they may actually race ahead of your pace in the process. They may run down the staircase, jump into the space shuttle and end up somewhere inside their body before you've even finished your words. So please make sure you keep up with them!

In children's work, we often ask an angel or hero to appear, rather than a mentor, as all children know what an angel or a hero is, and they trust their strength and wisdom.

Children are likely to have very vivid pictures of what it's like inside the body. It's delightful to give them time to describe it in detail. Be encouraging and engaged as they do so.

In the Change Memory process, please feel free to suggest some inner resources that might be useful to put in the balloons. Also, your child will remember the qualities that you discussed before the process, so they might like to choose some of these as well.

When it comes to forgiveness, children are generally quick to forgive. Before they do, make certain that they've expressed all the stored emotion. Encourage them to forgive only after they are empty.

If, after emptying out, for some reason they still feel unwilling to forgive (this is extremely rare!), simply ask their angel or hero 'What would have to happen in order to forgive?' The mentor will come up with the perfect solution. Let this happen at the camp-fire. Children are very creative and innovative in finding their own route to forgiveness and healing, but if you have any doubt at all – on any aspect of the process – just ask their mentor, angel or guide. Their own wisdom will easily come up with the answers appropriate to the situation.

Make certain that everyone at the campfire forgives everyone else – whether it's 'needed' or not. There's no harm in having an added dose of forgiveness.

When the campfire is over, give the child extra time to see how things are changing and transforming in their body. They love this part, and can be very descriptive.

Usually, when the process is complete, children feel impatient to get back into the space shuttle and go right back to the door, and often they *run* back up the stairs. Once again, let them go at their own pace.

Most Kids' Journeys last a maximum of 20 minutes, as children are quick to catch on to the process, find it easy to forgive, are quick to let go of old issues and are eager to finish. Please be sensitive to the pace your child wants to go at – it may be faster (or some-times even a little slower) than you might expect.

When they are completely complete, please make sure to congratulate your child: praise them, embrace them in your love. You might encourage them to draw or paint 'before' and 'after' pictures, and you might like to ask them how they will feel about their old issue in the future.

Generally speaking, kids feel so joyous and refreshed following their process work that they are eager to run out and play. It's good to let them celebrate their newfound energy and joy.

Sometimes during the process your child may open their eyes. There is no problem with this. Though I recommend that you encourage them to keep their eyes closed during the Kids' Journey process, it is not absolutely essential. Children have learned, through the process of listening to us reading fairytales, that they can imagine things fully with their eyes open. So while it's best for them to keep their eyes closed, it's not the end of the world if they pop open from time to time.

Most of all, trust yourself in working with your child. Know that they are already free, already whole. Deep inside is a shining diamond. All you are doing is clearing away a few layers, taking the lampshade off so that their own natural potential can begin to shine anew.

Remember, there is no greater tool or technique than the gift you brought with you when you purchased this book: your love for your child. '… and the greatest of these is love.'

To finish this chapter, I thought the following parent's letter would be an inspiration to all of us:

My son Tom was very shy and withdrawn and lacked confidence. He found comfort in the TV and the computer. He also did not fare too well in his oral exams at school, as he did not have the confidence to talk.

He attended The Journey workshop in Durban and my boy actually stood up and spoke in front of everyone at the workshop – without a stammer!

At school and at home he is confident and his self-esteem has grown. He even looks taller now, as before he would slouch, as if to become inconspicuous. He talks about The Journey to all his friends and has now become a 'mini counsellor' amongst his classmates. He wants to do this at school and start a Journey Club, as it has helped many of his friends whose parents have been through divorces or other traumas.

14

The Kids' Journey Process

Allow yourself to find a really comfortable position, and when you are ready, close your eyes … Now take a nice slow deep breath in … gently … Now let it out … and again, a nice slow deep breath in … and let it out … Good … And one more time … take a deep breath in … and let it out …

Now imagine receiving four really beautiful bright balloons filled with wonderful qualities … The first balloon is full of relaxation and peace, so, in your mind's eye, imagine taking this balloon of relaxation and peace … and now, breathing in that feeling … letting it fill your whole body … Good …

Next, imagine receiving a balloon of trust … Breathe in the trust … and let it fill your whole body … Good … Now a balloon of courage … Breathe that in … And now a balloon of fun … Breathe that in … Great …

So now that your whole body is filled with fun, courage, trust and relaxation, you can let the balloons disappear, knowing that all these qualities are already inside *you*.

Now imagine a beautiful downward-facing staircase with 10 magical shimmering steps ... This is a very special staircase, because it can carry you into a huge presence of love ... With each step you take, it carries you ever deeper into a vast presence of sparkling light ... And the good news is that you don't have to do a *thing* ... the steps do all the work ... All you have to do is step onto them and with every step, you'll find yourself relaxing ... naturally ... deeper and deeper ... into the presence of love and light in your core ...

So, can you see the staircase? ... Good ... Now, when you're ready, step onto step number 10 ... feeling yourself beginning to relax now ... now step 9 ... now 8 ... Great ... Notice how every step you take is *causing* you to *relax* and *open* more and more into the light and love ... 7 ... 6 ... 5 ... Feel your own energy beginning to expand now ... becoming spacious in front of you and vast behind ... Feel your own awareness growing vast and spacious on all sides ... 4 ... Feel relaxed and open ... and feel the room beginning to fill with light and love ... 3 ... 2 ... Feel a huge presence of love and peace surrounding you ... love inside ... love outside ... love everywhere ... 1 ... just resting now in an ocean of peace and love surrounding you and everything ...

In front of you is a big magical door ... Behind that door is a big bright light, full of love ... This is the light of your own deepest self ... Also behind the door is a special mentor or guide ... It might be a guardian angel or saint ... or perhaps even an action hero ... or even a very kind, wise wizard ... But it is someone whose wisdom you trust ... and someone in whose presence you feel very safe and protected ...

Can you see the door? ... Do you sense that there's a huge light behind it? ... Great ... Can you tell that there's someone kind and wise and safe just waiting there behind the door? ... Great ...

Now step through the doorway ... and feel yourself surrounded by bright light ... filled with love ... To the side is your mentor or guide ... Can you see your mentor? ... Great ... What are they like? ... Would you describe them to me? ... [Wait for description ... Be encouraging] ... Great ... Why don't you go right over to your guide and greet them? ...

Now, to the side of you is a beautiful, glistening space shuttle ... It's a very magical vehicle, because it can go very safely and gracefully *anywhere inside* your body ... and not only that, it knows *exactly* where it wants to go ... Can you see the space shuttle? ... Great ...

Now you and your guide can go ahead and step inside and shut the doors ... and strap on the seatbelts ... What's it like in there? ... [Wait for description ... Be encouraging] ... Great ...

There should be an amazing instrument panel in front of you ... and if you look closely, there's a green button ... When you're ready and all the doors are secure ... either you or your mentor can push the green button for lift-off ... You'll find that the space shuttle will carry you safely and easily to somewhere *inside* your body ... It can go into muscles, bones, organs, veins, the heart, eyes, ears, throat, blood or skin ... it can go *anywhere* inside the body ... and not only that, but *it knows exactly where* it wants to go because it's powered by your own body wisdom ... by the same part of you that makes your heart beat and your eyes shine and your breath go in and out ... So, when you are ready, you can push the green button ...

Have you pushed it? ... Good ... What's it like? ...

Now, slowly bring in your shuttle for a nice, gentle landing ... No crash landings please! ... and come to a complete safe stop ... [Let them describe] ...

Now, when you are ready, you can pull on the handbrake, take off your seatbelts and take out a torch or flashlight ... and step outside the shuttle ...

Begin shining your flashlight all around you as you step out and *feel* what it feels like under your feet ... What does it feel like? ... What does it look like in the area you've arrived in? ... Turn around and explore the whole area and describe it to me ... [Get lengthy description ... Be encouraging] ... Do you have a sense yet of where you might have arrived? ...

Notice that there is an area that is somehow *different* from the rest ... It might look darker or lighter ... or have a different texture or temperature or colour ...

Can you see that part ... and describe it to me?   Great ... Now, you and your mentor can go straight over to that area ... and, as you stand up next to it, all the feeling and emotion stored in that area will start pouring over you ... As you get really close to it, you will feel feelings beginning to pour over you ... If there were emotions coming from that area, I wonder what they might be? ... Just go there and stand right next to it and *feel* what you're beginning to feel right now ... Great ...

What is the feeling? ... Great ... Now ask yourself, 'When have I felt like this before?' and look straight down at your feet and, in your mind's eye, see what kind of shoes you might be wearing or not wearing, as you feel the emotion ... How old do you feel yourself to be? ... Ask yourself, 'When have I felt like this before?' ...

and in answer to that, look down at your feet and see what, if any, shoes you are wearing ... What are you wearing on your legs ... on your body? ... Are you inside the house or outside? ... Who else is there in the scene with you? ... How old do you feel your-self to be? ... What's beginning to take place in this old memory? ... Let the whole scene begin to play itself out ... the way it did back then, when you were younger ... and when you can really remember the entire scene, put the old memory up onto a big video screen in the sky ... and once it is up there, for now, let it go blank ... knowing that you can come back to it in a moment ...

Now you and your mentor can sit down next to a warm, cosy campfire filled with love and peace ... While sitting at this fire, you'll feel safe and you'll know that in a moment you're going to press the 'play' button on your remote control, and then together in the warm safety of this campfire, you and your guide can watch that old memory play on the video screen in the sky ... You can even sit in your mentor's lap if it makes you feel better ...

So, when you are ready, press the 'start' button and let that old scene play itself from beginning to end ... [Long pause] ... Have you done that? ... Great ...

Tell me what took place in that old memory ... Would you be will-

ing to describe it to me? ... [Wait for full description] ... Great ...
Now press the 'stop' button and let's invite the younger you who
was in that old memory to come and sit by the present-day you
and your mentor at the campfire ... So now there should be the
three of you sitting by the fire: the younger you, the present-day
you and your mentor ... Are you all there? ... Great ...

I wonder what inner qualities might have helped that younger you
cope better with that old memory? ... I wonder what kind of emotional resources might have been useful in that old scene? ... If
you look at your mentor, you'll see they are holding a big bouquet
of brightly coloured balloons ... In each balloon is a beautiful
inner quality that might have helped you in that old memory ... I
wonder what qualities might be in those balloons? ... What would
have helped you feel better *inside* in that old memory? ... What
kind of balloons would have been useful? ... [Let them name
some ... Be encouraging ... And then you might like to suggest
some that you feel would be appropriate ... Ask *if* they would like
to have any of your suggested balloons ...]

Now let's name each balloon, and when you let the younger you
receive a balloon, let them *breathe* that quality in ... and let it fill
their whole body ... So, one by one, let's go ahead and name the balloons ... Receive them and let your body fill up with that quality ...

[Take plenty of time, be fun and encouraging. Make sure they are inner qualities *not* external conditions!]

Now that the younger you is full of all these wonderful qualities, you can let the younger you step back onto the video screen in the sky ... only this time play the scene the way it *would have happened* with all these great inner qualities ... And now describe how the scene *would* have gone, if you'd had all these amazing qualities ... Play the scene the new, healthier, happier way, and then, when it's finished, let me know what happened ... [Let them describe in full ... Be encouraging ...]

Once the scene is complete and you've seen just how much easier and happier you felt inside with all your balloons ... let the younger you step back down off the screen and come back over to the campfire ... The younger you can sit in the lap of your mentor if it makes you feel better ... Now invite the other people from that scene to step down off the screen and come over to the campfire as well ...

So now everyone who was in that old memory should be sitting in the cosy warm presence of the fire ... Is the younger you there? ... Good ... The present-day you? ... Good ... Your mentor? ... Good ... All the other people from the scene? ... [Let them name each one ...] Wonderful ... So now everyone is sitting together at this cosy campfire ...

I'm sure the younger you has some old stored-up feelings that they would finally like to let out ... If there were some words that needed speaking, I wonder what they might be? ... Let the younger you *really* empty out all the pain and upset they felt at the time of that old memory ... and let the other people at the camp-fire finally just sit and listen ...

If the younger you could choose *one* person to speak to ... to finally get all their feelings off their chest, I wonder who the younger you might speak to? ... [Encourage them to pick the appropriate person ...]

Now is your time to get it all off your chest ... time for you to empty out all the words you never got a chance to speak ... If you could finally express the real truth of how you *really* felt in that old memory, what would the younger you say? ...

[Let the younger child express themselves fully. If they are having trouble letting the old emotions up and out, give them a balloon of the ability to feel and express emotions until empty.]

Now, knowing that the other person was probably doing the best they could with the pain they were in at that time ... if the other person could reply, not from their outer personality, but from a deeper, more truthful place inside ... what would the other person reply? ...

And if you could reply to them, what would you say to that? ... [Get full reply ...] And if the other person were to speak from their secret heart of hearts, what would they *really* say? What was going on emotionally at the time? ... Let them answer from their heart ... [Get reply ...] Good ... And what would you reply? ...

[Continue conversation like this until both parties are fully empty and have found some kind of peace and understanding.]

You might like to step inside that other person and feel what they were *really* feeling at that time ... [Let them describe ... Be encouraging ...]

Now step into that person's heart ... into the part of them that is full of love ... Now, from their heart of hearts, from the very best part of them ... look out through their eyes and see how loving and kindly they *really* felt towards you at that time.

Now step outside that other person ... If that person could speak *now*, what would they say? ... Would they say they're sorry and they wish they hadn't hurt you? ... And what might you reply to that? ... Would you be willing to accept their apology? ... Great ...

Now ask the mentor if there is anything else that needs to be said or expressed ...

If the present-day you could finally say something to the other person, what would you say? ... And if the other person could respond from the same place, deeper inside, what would they reply? ... Let both of you finally open up and express everything ... [Keep emptying out until finished ...]

Now that you've had a chance to really empty out all that stored pain and hurt, I wonder if you might be willing to forgive that other person? ... [Let them answer ...] Even though you cannot excuse their previous behaviour, are you willing to finally let them apologize and forgive them? ... Great ...

Let them say 'I'm sorry' and you can say you're sorry, too ... And now you can forgive them completely ... You can do that out loud ...

[You can repeat this whole process with one other person at the campfire if needed.]

Then, sending everyone at the campfire your love and forgiveness, and with the prayer that they finally forgive themselves, you can let all the other people disappear into the light ... Now there's just the younger you, the present-day you and your mentor left ... Is it just the three of you now? ... Great ...

Now, turn to the younger you and say, 'I'm sorry you went through so much pain ... You just didn't have access to all the beautiful inner qualities that I do now ... I promise you will *never* go through that previous pain again ... because from now on *I* will love and protect you' ... Then, handing the younger you their big bouquet of balloons ... let the younger you fill up with all the wonderful inner qualities ... breathing them in ... letting them fill their whole body ...

Now hug the younger you, and let the younger you melt right into the present-day you ... becoming part of you ... growing up now, with all these wonderful internal qualities ... right inside *you*! ... Feel the younger you growing up to be the you *now* ... and breathe in all the fabulous qualities, knowing that they are now part of your body, your being ... They are in your cells ...

Now it's time to let the campfire disappear ... and you and your mentor can walk around that area you first arrived in ... inside your body ... Notice how things are beginning to change there now ... How much shinier, brighter and fresher are things now?

… Would you tell me how that whole area looks now? … [Wait for full description … Be encouraging] … Describe that area that used to be somehow different … What does it look like now? … How is it changing now? … Walk around and *really* describe how everything is healing there now …

If that part of your body had any final advice it would like to give you, what might it say? … What might it want you to know? …

Now it's time to get back into your space shuttle, grateful that the same part of you that makes your heart beat will continue the healing process naturally, on its own, without you having to think about it …

Are you back in your shuttle? … OK … Close the doors, strap on the seatbelts and push the green button again … Let the shuttle carry you back to the original doorway you first came through …

Are you there yet? … Great … Now say goodbye to your mentor, knowing that you can go on another internal Journey again any time you like … [Give time …] Is there any final advice your mentor wants to give you? … OK, then give them a big hug …

Then turn to the door and walk back through, knowing that you can greet your mentor again on your next Journey ... and look at the 10 steps shining in front of you ... Feel all the light and love surrounding you ... Let the light and love fill your entire being ...

Now step onto step 1 ... step 2 ... knowing that with every step you take, you're coming back into the full wholeness and joy of the present moment ... 3 ... 4 ... 5 ... feeling relaxed, refreshed and grateful you went on this internal Journey ... 6 ... 7 ... happy that you have all your balloon qualities inside your body ... filling your very cells ... and feeling grateful that you forgave ... 8 ... 9 ... and when you step onto step 10, you'll find you'll only be able to open your eyes as soon as all parts of you are fully complete, ready to carry on the healing perfectly, naturally, on their own ... And when all parts of you have decided to heal, you'll find when I say '10', you will be able to open your eyes ... 10 ... You may open your eyes ...

Excellent job! ... Well done! ... You did an amazing process ...

[Give time. Be very encouraging, full of praise. Make sure they remember all their balloons. Let them know how amazing they were and what a privilege it was to work with them.]

15

Working with Teenagers

Though this is not a book about working with teenagers, I'm sure you'll recognize its potential and might feel inclined to work with your teenage kids. So I'd like to make a few suggestions that we have found useful in working with these young adults.

Generally speaking, once a child is 13 years old, I feel they have enough inner wisdom to fully understand and undergo the adults' Emotional Journey and Physical Journey processes. So I usually suggest that your teenager reads the original adult book *The Journey*. In it are in-depth teachings and instructions for a full Emotional Journey process (something not covered in this kids' book), and it really does get you in touch with your own soul – with the wisdom and peace inside.

Because it is such in-depth work, I really feel it's up to each individual whether they want to undergo it or not. If, after reading the book, your teenager feels they might like to give it a shot, one way they might do it is to find a friend, relative or therapist and *process the* other *person first*. Then they can swap and let themselves be processed.

The reason I suggest this is that it puts your teenager at ease with the process and puts the partner on an *equal footing* with them. Often for teenagers this is a very big deal. They don't like to feel that some adult is trying to 'fix' them. However, if there will be an equal swap, i.e. both people will have to open their hearts equally, both will bare their souls and neither will be setting themselves up as some expert, then your teenager may feel that the situation is fair and healthy and be more open to giving it a try. Even exchanging process work with their peers is preferable to adults 'lording' the process over them and coercing them into something they would rather not do.

In Soweto, Journeywork is hugely successful with teenagers aged 14 to 18. All have read *The Journey* and they do regular Journey swaps with other teenagers in their groups. It's viewed as being fun, spiritual and healthy, and these young adults are models of self-confidence, character and inner strength.

If *you* feel inclined to do the work, which I pray you do, I recommend that you too read the original Journey book. As parents, the greatest example we can give to our kids and teenagers is to admit that we too have issues and to actively open our hearts, clear out our own blocks and come to a place of wholeness and peace in ourselves. In this way, as an entire family we are serving one another in finding our own light, opening up to our own true potential and expressing our own magnificence. Everyone recognizes that we all have our 'stuff' and that, more importantly, true freedom can be found within ourselves.

My deepest prayer is that there is healing among all families and that each and every human soul discovers the extraordinary presence of Grace inside us all.

May we all take the lampshades off our light and liberate our shining potential.

Gratitude

First, my heartfelt thanks to the children whose stories fill these pages. Their innocence completely disarms us, their wisdom inspires us and their capacity for healing seems endless. Thank you for opening us all to the possibilities of true awakening and self-discovery. You know who you are, and though your names have been changed, please accept all of my gratitude for your courage. May we all discover the freedom and wholeness you so effortlessly uncovered through your Journeys.

My deep gratitude to the teachers and therapists who, with great courage, took this work into schools, youth groups, teen development groups and social organizations. You are real-life models of possibility and you will truly make a difference in all of our futures by helping our children liberate their shining potential.

Special thanks to Carole Hart, Kim Davis and Jayshree Mannie, schoolteachers who not only took the work into schools but are now offering the Kids' Journey programmes in the UK, South

Africa and Australia. Also to Sally Matthews, a deeply caring therapist who has lovingly given the Junior Journey workshop in the
UK over the last few years. Thank you, Kim, for designing creative
and useful teachers' aids, so that other teachers are supported in
using the work in the classroom. Also, thank you to Angie
Jamieson for lovingly offering Journeywork to teenagers in youth
programmes in Soweto, South Africa.

My whole heart goes to Jayshree Mannie, who first took The
Journey into a school in South Africa and who is now taking the
work into underprivileged communities – to people who could
not otherwise afford this teaching. With great love, joy and dedi-
cation, Jayshree carries the work into social organizations, adult
groups, abuse programmes, Child-Line, Lifeline, etc. Wherever
help and healing are needed, Jayshree offers The Journey.
Currently, at the behest of the South African educational department, she is teaching 75 schoolteachers how to use the Kids'
Journey in the classroom. She is also training private-school
teachers in the work. Thank you, thank you, Jayshree. You are an
inspiration to us all through your work. By giving so many children the chance to fully experience their true potential, you will
surely help liberate your country.

Thank you to the countless parents, uncles, aunts, Journey
Accredited Therapists and Journey grads from all over the world

who sent in their beautiful stories of healing. Though we couldn't include every one of them, you are still an inspiration to us all.

Special thanks go to The Journey team – our deeply caring staff and trainers who support people worldwide in awakening and healing. Your hearts are so pure and each of you goes way beyond the call of duty to serve humanity. One of the greatest blessings in my life is the fierce love of Truth that all of you share. You are models of commitment and courage. So many people support The Journey that I could not begin to name all of them, but I'd like to personally thank our immediate staff, Gaby and Cliff Burt, Laurie Siemers, Jess McLeod, Tricia Hudson, Claire Butler, Vanessa, Szychter, Dean Pirera, Deb Burgess, Sarah Burnard, Lydia Garrow, Caryl Morgan, Sharon Johnson, Sudesh Mannie, and Kristine and Skip Lackey.

Once again I find myself feeling blessed by my radiant and inspired editor Carole Tonkinson. Through your inspiration and guidance this book was transformed from a kids' book into a parenting book, so that parents all over the world could be allowed to partner their children in their healing Journeys. I feel graced to have an editor with such wisdom and vision.

My deepest thanks to my partner Kevin Billett. Kevin truly partners me in all writing. He is at once both my muse and my editor. He is my sounding-board and my inspiration. Kevin meticulously and tirelessly pours over every word, making certain it carries the truth, integrity and potency intended. This book was co-authored as our joint work of love.

And, ultimately, the real co-author is Grace itself. With all my being I thank Grace. May every breath be breathed, every moment be lived as a never-ending prayer of gratitude in service to Truth.

BRANDON BAYS

Author's Note

With all my heart I pray that the children's joyous stories of healing and liberation have inspired you to partner your child in their
healing Journeys. I hope the simple and practical processes will
become a natural part of your parenting skills and that you will
feel free to use them alongside whatever other empowering and
healing techniques you've already learned.

Perhaps your child may even inspire you to go on *your* own personal Journey to liberate your own shining potential. Then,
together, you can partner each other in taking the lampshades off
your lights.

If you feel called to go further with this work and would like to
know more about kids' workshops, adult seminars and other
Journey products, please call The Journey 'warm line':

United Kingdom: +44 (0)7000 783646 or +44 (0)1656 890400

Australia: +61 (0)2 6685 9989 or +61 1 300 30 44 14

South Africa: +27 (0) 86 110 2223

USA: +1 866 860 0900

You can access our website at: www.thejourney.com
or email us at: info@thejourney.com

Our website is chock-full of useful information, including our international schedule and the names and contact details of Journey Accredited Therapists in your area.

Finally, if you'd like to begin your Journey in freedom and liberate your shining potential, I strongly recommend you read *The Journey: An Extraordinary Guide for Healing your Life and Setting Yourself Free* (Thorsons, 1999).

There are also CDs, tapes, products and services available to support you in continuing your Journey. Please contact us personally at the Journey office. You'll find very warm and welcoming Accredited Therapists there who will gently support you in any aspect of your healing Journey.

May you truly liberate your own shining potential.

BRANDON BAYS

The Journey

Brandon Bays

*An Extraordinary Guide for Healing Your Life
and Setting Yourself Free*

In 1992, Brandon Bays was diagnosed with a football-sized tumour and found herself catapulted into a remarkable, soul-searching and ultimately freeing healing journey. Only six and a half weeks later, she was pronounced textbook perfect – no drugs, no surgery, no tumour.

The profound original process of self-healing that Brandon Bays pioneered has since freed thousands from lifelong emotional and physical blocks. Through the unique work detailed in this book, she shares her deeply transformative techniques:

☼ Strip away years of emotional and physical blocks
☼ Tap into your own inner genius
☼ Live your life as an expression of your highest potential
☼ Experience the boundless joy within
☼ Become truly free